Honey In The Rock

by

Bud Robinson

First Fruits Press
Wilmore, Kentucky
c2015

Honey in the Rock, by Bud Robinson.

First Fruits Press, ©2015
Previously published: Cincinnati, Ohio: God's Revivalist Press, ©1913

ISBN: 9781621712060 (print), 9781621712077 (digital), 9781621712084 (kindle)

Digital version at http://place.asburyseminary.edu/firstfruitsheritagematerial/99/

For all other uses, contact:

First Fruits Press
B.L. Fisher Library
Asbury Theological Seminary
204 N. Lexington Ave.
Wilmore, KY 40390
http://place.asburyseminary.edu/firstfruits

Robinson, Bud, 1860-1942.
    Honey in the rock / by Bud Robinson.
    288 pages ; 21 cm.
    Wilmore, Ky. : First Fruits Press, ©2015.
    Reprint. Previously published: Cincinnati, Ohio: God's Revivalist Press, ©1913.
    ISBN: 978621712060 (pbk.)
    1. Holiness -- Sermons. I. Title.
BX7990.H6 R6 2015   234.8

Cover design by Amelia Hegle

asburyseminary.edu
800.2ASBURY
204 North Lexington Avenue
Wilmore, Kentucky 40390

First Fruits
THE ACADEMIC OPEN PRESS OF ASBURY SEMINARY

First Fruits Press
The Academic Open Press of Asbury Theological Seminary
204 N. Lexington Ave., Wilmore, KY 40390
859-858-2236
first.fruits@asburyseminary.edu
asbury.to/firstfruits

BROTHER BUD ROBINSON AND FAMILY

HONEY IN THE ROCK

BY

BUD ROBINSON

*Author of: "Sunshine and Smiles," "Story of Lazarus,"
"A Pitcher of Cream," Etc.*

GOD'S REVIVALIST PRESS
Ringgold, Young and Channing Sts.
CINCINNATI OHIO, U. S. A.

To all the people of America that can read, and to those who are going to learn to read later on in this life, I send out this new book, "Honey in the Rock," hoping that it may find a place on your shelves, and that you will read it until you get the back so dirty that you will have to have it rebound. It is just what its name indicates— honey in the Rock, and I give you my word there are no dead bees in the book; every bee is a working bee, no drones, not one, to be found. As I wrote the book, the Lord and the devil know that my bees swarmed a number of times, but for every swarm of bees I found a hundred acres of redtop clover, and I want you to have one old, fat bee-gum full of honey in the backyard of your soul that you have not robbed this summer, and in a case of immergency you can rob your bees. I wonder if you catch on?

Lovingly,

Bud Robinson.

CONTENTS.

Chapter I.

Why I Believe in Scriptural Holiness.

Dear reader, I would love to just sit down and have a quiet talk with you, and tell you just why I believe in scriptural holiness. Now the question will naturally rise in the mind of a fellow, Why do I believe this doctrine? The most of the people reject it, and men of brains reject it, and even great preachers reject it, and then, who am I that I should believe such a doctrine? Now that is one way that plenty of good men will reason about it, and if we were to look at the people we would drift like the great bulk of them are drifting, and if we were to undertake to accept the opinions of the people, we would believe everything that is above ground, for the crowd that don't accept the doctrine is not agreed between themselves. No two of them advocate the same thing or the same theory, and we are driven to the Bible for our doctrine, and we are frank to say that if the Bible don't teach it, that we won't want it, it makes no difference how reasonable it might appear on the surface. But we believe that the old Book teaches it as clearly as the rainbow and as beautifully.

Now for a text we want to read First Peter 3: 15: "But sanctify the Lord God in your hearts: and be ready always to give an answer to every man that asketh you a reason of the hope that is in you with meekness and fear." Now here the reader will notice that we are to sanctify the Lord God in our hearts, and the word "sanctify" don't mean to justify, or it don't mean to regenerate, or it don't mean to pardon; it means to *sanctify*. And then he said, "Be ready always to give an answer to every man that asketh you a reason of the hope that is in you." And now I am ready to give the reason just why I believe in the doctrine of scriptural holiness.

I mean by scriptural holiness the experience of sanctification as a second work of grace received by faith instantaneously, and I want to stretch out the word and make it as long as your arm, but I want you to get the blessing in a minute. Now my first reason why I believe in the doctrine is because it is an old doctrine, and not a new idea under the sun, as some want to try to make us believe. In proof of the fact that it is an old doctrine, we will read Eph. 1:4: "According as He hath chosen us in Him before the foundation of the world, that we should be holy and without blame before Him in love." Now, reader, there is no way of going back any further, and when we trace holiness back before the foundation of the world we have gotten back as far as we can go and keep our heads. That don't look much like a new doctrine, does it? It is old as the foundation of the earth, and the world don't look new to a country boy.

The text says that it was God's choice before the foundation of the world that we should be holy. It is perfectly natural to think of God as a holy God, and then it is perfectly natural to think of a holy God desiring His people to be like Himself, and as Heaven is the home of God and we are to stay with Him in His home, it is perfectly natural to think of God wanting us to be in perfect harmony with Him and His home and His government, and if we could get into Heaven without holiness, we would be out of harmony with God, and therefore as miserable as if we were in the pit. It is strange to me when I think of some people that I have met, that told

me that they were Christians and on their way
to Heaven, and at the same time they could not
stand a little Holiness meeting in this world. I
wondered what they would do in Heaven where
there is nothing but holiness.

Now, reader, you may not agree with me
as to what I say about holiness, but you must
agree with the Lord and also with the Bible,
and when the Bible tells us it was God's choice
before the foundation of the world that we should
be holy, it is up to us to say, "Yes, Lord," and go
down after it and lose no time, either, for Christ
said, "Walk while you have the light, for the
night cometh when no man can work."

Now we come to the next reason for believing
in scriptural holiness. We read in First Thess.
4:3: "For this is the will of God, even your
sanctification." Now, brother, we have seen
that it was God's choice before the foundation
of the world that we should be holy, and now we
have before us the fact that it is God's will that
we should be sanctified, and His choice and His
will ought to be in perfect harmony with each
other and I believe that they are. Brother or
sister, if the great God put it in His will that you
are to be wholly sanctified, and you refuse to let

Him do it for you, doesn't it look to you like you are out of harmony with God? How "can two walk together except they be agreed?" says the old Bible, and if God willed you the blessing of sanctification and you refuse to let Him sanctify you, doesn't that look a little dangerous and a little shaky to you? Hadn't you better reconsider that thing before it is too late? If God says, "Come," and we refuse to come, after while God will say, "Go," and we will go. I tell you, man, when God says, "Come," we had better come, and when God says, "Woe," we had better woe. When God says, "Come," there is always something good awaiting us, and when God says, "Woe," there is danger. The most blessed thing that God ever said was, "Come unto Me," and the most awful thing that God ever said was, "Depart from Me," and, friends, we will come or we will go. If it is God's will that I should be sanctified, that settles it, so far as I am concerned; I will go to Him to have His will wrought out in me.

"For this is the will of God, even your sanctification," is about the most interesting thing that a man ever listened to, when we think of the fact that it is holiness or it is Hell, one or the other, and God will never trim things to suit the taste of men or women who would rather have a night in the ballroom or a night in the lodge than a night with God in prayer.

Well, now we have come to the next reason why we believe in scriptural holiness. First it was God's choice and second it was God's will. Now we turn to First Peter 1:15, 16: "But as He which hath called you is holy, so be ye holy in all manner of conversation; because it is written, Be ye holy, for I am holy." Now here, reader, we see that God has put it into His law and commanded us to be holy, and the only reason that He gave was "Because I am holy." Those were His words and not mine, and He meant it, and we have to meet it at the judgment bar of God. Think of it—His choice, His will and His command, that we should be holy, and then men even preach against it and say that the Bible doesn't teach it. Are they blind or are they deceived by the devil? What is the matter with a man in the face of God's eternal Word? How can they teach such doctrine when we have just read that it was God's choice before the foundation of the world that we shoud be holy, and we have just read that "This is the will of God, even your sanctification," and now we read, "Be ye holy, for I the Lord your God am holy"?

Here it is up to us to take holiness or to meet God without it, one or the other. We can't think of a holy God giving a command to His people to be unholy, but we can think of a holy God giving a command to His people to be holy. We know another thing, we know that the God that is revealed in the Bible loves holiness and hates sin, and we know that the devil that is revealed in the Bible hates holiness and loves sin, and just in proportion as we love holiness and hate sin, or love sin and hate holiness are we like God or like the devil. Again, we can't think of a holy God commanding us to be any other way but holy, for if He did it would put us out of harmony with Him and there would be no fellowship between us and Him.

No longer ago than yesterday I met a Methodist preacher on the streets, and he is not a believer in holiness. He has opposed it openly and thrown his influence against it, and when we met there was no fellowship between us; he seemed to be perfectly miserable in my presence and wanted to get away, and was so nervous and

restless that he got out of my sight as quickly as
he could.   I was a perfect stranger to the man,
we had never met before; I was a thousand
miles from home and had been called by the good
people of the town to hold a meeting.   The difference was, no heart fellowship between us, and
that will be the trouble with the unsanctified at
the Judgment Day, no fellowship between them
and God.

Our next reason for believing in scriptural
holiness is found in Acts 20: 32: "And now,
brethren, I commend you to God, and the word
of His grace, which is able to build you up,
and to give you an inheritance among all them
which are sanctified."   Now the reader will notice that you have to be an heir before you can
have an inheritance, and it takes the new birth
to make you an heir; no sinner or even a backslider is an heir to the experience of sanctification.   The sinner has to be born again to make
him an heir, and the backslider has to be re-
claimed to be a fit subject for the experience of
holiness.   The people that Saint Paul addressed
were brethren, or Christians, and he said that
their inheritance was the blessing of sanctification, and that proves the two works of grace,

because you must be born of the Spirit before
you could be baptized with the Spirit. · In the
above text Paul tells the brethren that their inheritance was the blessing of sanctification; they
were not sinners, they were brethren beloved of
the Lord; and they were not backslidden, they
were fit subjects for the experience of scriptural
holiness just as I am a-preaching it.

The very fact that God will provide such an
experience for the children of men proves at
least two things: first, it proves that they need
it, and second, it proves that we can get it, for
it would have been a foolish thing for our blessed
heavenly Father to have provided something for
us that we could not get, and yet some good people seem to think that we can never get the blessing while we live. There is but very little said
in the Bible about what we shall do in Heaven,
but nobody has any trouble in believing that we
will be holy up there, but they don't think that
Christ can make them holy down in this world.
But it must be remembered that when the Son
of God started back to Heaven, He said, "All
power is given unto Me in Heaven and in earth."
If that is so (and we know it is), there is no room
for a man to doubt, for if Christ has all power

in Heaven and in earth, then anything that He
can do for a man in Heaven He can do for him
in earth.   If the man on earth will yield himself to the hand of the blessed Savior, He can
first convert him and blot out all his sins, and
second He can sanctify him wholly and preserve
him blameless until He returns in the clouds to
catch away His waiting Bride.   That is all Book
also, and I believe every word of it from the deep
of my soul.

When the dear old apostle said, "And now,
brethren, I commend you to God and the word
of His grace, which is able to build you up and
to give you an inheritance among all them which
are sanctified," I believe that I am one of the
brethren, and that it means me, and I am a-going to my Father and tell Him that I have come
after my inheritance, for I am an heir and there
is no law in Heaven or in earth that can beat a
lawful heir out of his estate.   When I was born
into the heavenly family, I then and there became
an heir, and to-day I rejoice in the fact that we
have the greatest doctrine in the known world.
Of course it does not belong to me more than
it does to any other man, but if the other fellow
rejects it and I accept it, there is a big difference between me and him, for he is a rejecter,

and I am an accepter; I have it, and he hasn't it, that is the difference.

Now, dear reader, we have come to the next reason why we believe in scriptural holiness. We have noticed that it was God's choice and God's will and God's command, and our birthright, and now we come to Heb. 13: 12: "Wherefore Jesus also, that He might sanctify the people with His own blood, suffered without the gate." Now here we offer as one of our reasons why we believe in scriptural holiness the fact that the blessed Son of God suffered without the gate that He might sanctify the people with His own blood. This is one of the best reasons for believing in scriptural holiness that I ever saw, and it is up to me to get sanctified or reject the blood of the Son of God, one or the other; it is up to me to either accept it or reject it, and when a man rejects the blood of the Son of God he is not rejecting man, but God. I fear that millions of people will go up to the judgment bar of God a-thinking that they had only rejected man's idea of things, and find out, when it is too late, that they had been rejecting the blood of the blessed Son of God, and had not rejected man at all. So, brother, we must stand or fall by the old Book.

Now, dear reader, we could go on and pile up many words, and could write for the next hour on the above text, but don't you see that all we might say would not strengthen the Bible? If the blessed Son of God suffered without the gate that He might sanctify the people with His own blood, I am going to give you that as a good reason for believing the doctrine of holiness, and no man can reason the text out of the Bible. To deny it, don't answer the Book at all, and as sure as we live, the old Book is true, and by its teaching we will stand or by its teaching we will fall. It is light that graduates guilt, and when God turns on the light it is for us to walk in and not to reject. If our Father loved us well enough to provide the blessing of sanctification for us, we at least ought to accept it and praise Him while we have breath for His goodness to us, for we read, you know, that "without holiness no man shall see the Lord," and we believe that God meant just what He said and said just what He meant, and we must be holy, for we all want to see Him and I must see Him.

I now come to the next reason why I believe in scriptural holiness. We have seen that it was God's choice, and God's will, and God's command, and your birthright, and that Jesus died that

you might have it, and now we turn to Heb.
10: 14-16: "For by one offering He hath perfected for ever them that are sanctified. Whereof
the Holy Ghost also is a witness to us: for after
that He had said before, This is the covenant
that I will make with them after those days, saith
the Lord, I will put My laws into their hearts,
and in their minds will I write them." Now the
seventeenth verse says, "And their sins and iniquities will I remember no more." Now the reader
will notice that in the tenth verse He says that
"by one offering He hath perfected for ever them
that are sanctified." Now, beloved, He don't
say them that are justified, and He don't say them
that are regenerated, but He does say them that
are sanctified. Now here is the best Baptist and
Presbyterian doctrine in the Bible, and, as a general thing, they both reject it. This is the only
passage of Scripture that says they have got it
forever. How strange it seems to a fellow that
has his eyes open that they will tell you that
they have it, and can't lose it, and at the same
time tell you that they haven't got it! They
make me think of the man that was so badly
cross-eyed that when he wept the tears went
down his back, and their lives are so crooked
that they would make you think of the man that

had such a crooked nose that when he blew his
nose he knocked a fly off of the top of his ear.
Now that looks like the fellow that don't believe
in the doctrine of scriptural holiness, and at the
same time tells you that he can't lose what he
has got, and you wonder if he has anything from
the way he is living.

But you notice that God said that by one
offering He had perfected forever them that are
sanctified, then He adds, "whereof the Holy
Ghost is also a witness unto us." Now the reader
will notice that we have got the blessing forever
and that the Holy Ghost witnesses to it, so,
after all, it is not a perpetual going on and never
getting there, for the Holy Ghost could not witness to a thing that could not be performed.
If holiness is a perpetual going on unto, as the
preachers in many places tell us, of course the
Holy Ghost could not witness to it. When a
man repents of his sins, confesses his sins, forsakes his sins and believes on the Lord Jesus
Christ, God then and there gives him an instan-
taneous pardon. Pardon is not a perpetual going on, but a work of grace wrought in the
heart of man in a moment of time when he meets
God's conditions, and so it is with the blessing
of sanctification, it comes instantaneously and

the man knows that it is done. Glory to God in the highest, and on earth peace and good will toward men!

In the fourteenth verse we see that we are sanctified forever, and in the fifteenth we see that the Holy Ghost witnesses to it, and in the sixteenth we see that God makes a covenant with us and writes His laws down in our hearts and minds, and in the seventeenth we notice that we are to get rid of our sins and our iniquities. The reader will notice two things in that seventeenth verse—our sins and our iniquities. Now don't you see that when we got converted we got rid of our sins, and when we got sanctified we got rid of our iniquities? There are two works of grace just as plain and as reasonable as anything on earth can be. They are not big enough or plain enough to cover up a man's prejudice, but they will cover the soul of every honest man, give him victory through the blood of the blessed Son of God, and make him an overcomer, and then his life will be victorious; he will have a level head, and a big soul, and a good heart, and a sweet experience, and a loving disposition, and a kind word, and a big smile, and a hearty handshake for the fellow that needs it, and that will enable him to read his title clear to the mansion

in the sky. So I am very glad that God does
sanctify a man, and make him perfect, and give
him the Holy Ghost to witness to it, and then
makes the covenant with him, and writes His
laws down in the man's heart and in his mind,
and then remembers his sins and his iniquities
no more.

Now, brother, to me that is one of the best
reasons for believing in scriptural holiness that
I think I ever saw; I don't see how you could
improve on it. That Scripture is as deep as the
demand of fallen humanity, as broad as the compassion of God, as high as Heaven, and as everlasting as the Rock of Ages. No room there for
doubts, no room there for complaint, no place
there for sore heads, no place there for grumb-
lers, but a mighty fine place for those who have
been pardoned, and sanctified, and filled with all
the fullness of God, and with their souls a-shining through their faces and a-weeping with their
eyes and a-laughing with their mouths, at the
same time they are the greatest set of folks on
the dirt to-day to see a man or a woman, as the
case may be, in a big Holiness meeting, a-weeping just like their hearts would break and
a-laughing just like they were tickled to death
about something, and all of this a-going on at

the same time. What a wonderful combination a wholly sanctified man is anyway! He is a walking curiosity and a puzzle to the devil, and a wonder to the angels of light. I saw a man get his house burned down once and it was so terrible to him that it took a man or two to hold him, but a few years later my nephew by marriage got his house burned down and everything that he had was consumed, and the neighbors told me that he shouted all the time while it burned, but he has the blessing and he has it good, and he got it by the second-blessing route.

Dear reader, we now come to our next reason for believing in scriptural holiness. You may turn now and read Heb. 2: 11: "For both He that sanctifieth and they who are sanctified are all of one, for which cause He is not ashamed to call them brethren." Now, reader, if you really have the blessing, your friends and even the members of your own household may be ashamed of you, but there is one glorious consolation, and it is this, that your heavenly Father will not be ashamed of you. There is one city where every man and woman and child is in the experience of scriptural holiness; there is not a man there that smokes tobacco, there is not a spittoon in the city and there is no lodge there,

there is no such a thing as the man of the house
a-staying out till a late hour of the night while
his wife walks the floor and rocks the cradle
and says, "How long, O Lord, how long!"

I am frank to confess that in the average
church of our day it takes more courage and
backbone to stand up in the church and testify
to the experience of scriptural holiness than anything else that a Christian can be called on to
do. I know of but one thing now that is really
unpopular in the average church, and that is
to be a true, scriptural holiness man and stand
up and witness to it in the presence of the people, but, after all, God is not ashamed of the sanctified man, for the text said that "Both He that
sanctifieth and they who are sanctified are all of
one, for which cause He is not ashamed to call
them brethren." Notice first that "He that sanctifieth." That shows that God does it for us.
And notice, "they who are sanctified." That
shows that somebody has got it. Notice again,
"are all of one." There is a holy union between
God and the sanctified soul. And now notice,
"and for this cause He is not ashamed to call
them brethren." Now, reader, I think that that
is a good reason for believing in scriptural holiness. Of course you may not, but I do, and I
thank the Lord that I do believe it.

Now, reader, we have come to our last reason for believing in scriptural holiness that we will give you in this discourse. You may turn to Heb. 12: 14: "Follow peace with all men, and holiness, without which no man shall see the Lord." Now, in your mind, just turn back and review the reasons that I have given you for believing in scriptural holiness, and see if you don't think that I am reasonable. First, we saw that it was God's choice (Eph. 1: 4); second, we saw that it was God's will (1 Thess. 4: 3); third, we saw that it was God's command (1 Pet. 1: 15, 16); fourth, we saw that it was our birthright (Acts 20: 32); fifth, we saw that Jesus died that we might have it (Heb. 13: 12); sixth, we saw that the Holy Ghost witnesses to it (Heb. 10: 14-16); seventh, we saw that God was not ashamed of a sanctified man (Heb. 2: 11); and eighth, we see that we can't see God without it (Heb. 12: 14).

Now in a hurried way I have run over these reasons for believing in scriptural holiness, and I have asked the people all over these United States that don't believe in holiness as a second work of grace to give me eight reasons from the Bible why they don't believe in it, and so far not one of them has ever given me a single rea-

son, and I am going to say here that there is
not a man on earth that can prove that men
ever get sanctified by any other process than by
a second work of grace. There are a few tobacco-soaked preachers that claim that they got
it all at once. Well, they evidently did get all
that they ever did get all at once, for they don't
seem to have gotten anything for the last gen-
eration. When you can smell a preacher as he
goes by, he is, at the best construction that you
can put on him, awful bad off. And even if
we grow into it, or get it when we die, or get
it in Purgatory, or get it at the general Judgment Day, it is a second blessing, and so everything in the universe is on our side when it is
boiled down and skimmed. I have many more
reasons, but these will satisfy any reasonable
man.

CHAPTER II.
THE ABUNDANT SUPPLY.

Dear reader, you will find the text for this discourse in the ninth chapter of Second Corinthians, and the eighteenth verse: "And God is able to make all grace abound toward you; that ye, always having all sufficiency in all things, may abound to every good work." Now, the reader will notice that in the above text God has put Himself on record as being able to make all grace abound toward you, and the question naturally arises in the mind of the man of our day, "Can He do it?" And men halt, and wonder, and doubt, and look wise, and feel big, and turn away, and say, "We will hear thee again concerning this matter." But I want to take this ground and affirm that "God *IS* able to make all grace abound toward you; that ye, always having all sufficiency in all things, may abound to every good work." And I want to say further on this subject that everything that you need to make you pure and holy and kind and

23

good and Christlike and loving and gentle God
has an abundance of for you. And now I affirm
that it is up to me to prove it by the blessed
old Book, and by the grace of our God, I can
do it, and make it so plain that anybody that will
look can see it.

Now what is the first thing that we need
to make us just what we ought to be? Well,
I believe that you will agree with me that the
first thing that we need is the mercy of God;
not His justice, not His wrath, not His law,
but His mercy. Without the mercy of God we
are ruined forever and ever, but with His mercy
we are saved from His justice and His wrath.
Don't you see that when we sin against God
His justice would cut us down and His wrath
would put us in the pit of eternal despair? So
we are agreed that the first thing that a lost
world needs is the mercy of a loving heavenly
Father.

Now turn with me to First Peter and read
from the second verse to the fifth verse of the
first chapter and you will see that God has abundance of mercy for us, and that is the thing
that we need. "Elect according to the foreknowledge of God the Father, through sanctification of the Spirit, unto obedience and sprink-

ling of the blood of Jesus Christ: Grace unto
you, and peace, be multiplied. Blessed be the
God and Father of our Lord Jesus Christ, which
according to His abundant mercy hath begotten
us again unto a lively hope by the resurrection
of Jesus Christ from the dead, to an inheritance
incorruptible, and undefiled, and that fadeth not
away, reserved in Heaven for you, who are kept
by the power of God through faith unto salvation ready to be revealed in the last time."

Now the reader will notice that I have made
a very long quotation here, and it is in order
that you might get the full light of this beautiful Scripture. You can't find five more beautiful verses in the Bible than the above, and the
point that I want you to see is brought out in
the third verse where the apostle uses the words
"abundant mercy." Now, brother, God is too
good and too wise to provide anything for us that
we do not need, and the very fact that God provided abundance of mercy for us proves to me
that we are in great need and hopelessly lost
without it. So the first thing we need is mercy
and here is an abundance of it for us. That is
the first thing that we need and here is all we
need of it. We can lie down and wallow in the
mercy of God, and get up and shake ourselves

and splash and swim in it like the boys in the swimming-hole down in the creek behind the old farm.

But we need more than mercy to get us out of the life of sin. Mercy is the first step and leads to the second step, which is pardon. Now we will turn to the prophecy of Isaiah, and read 55:6, 7: "Seek ye the Lord while He may be found, call ye upon Him while He is near: let the wicked forsake his way, and the unrighteous man his thoughts: and let him return unto the Lord, and He will have mercy upon him; and to our God, for He will abundantly pardon."

The leading thought in the above verses is this, the abundance of pardon. First we had the abundance of mercy, that is the first thing that we need, and the second thing that we need is pardon, and here we find that God has provided abundance of it for us. The reason is because we are guilty, and a guilty man is a lost man without he gets mercy and pardon. Without it he is lost and with it he is saved, and, thank God! He has all we need of it. We can just help ourselves, and walk in the light, and shine and shout and praise Him for His goodness to us, for being so thoughtful of us when we had forgotten our own selves. Just see us as help-

less as a mortal could be, lost and we did not
know that we were lost, and blind and we did
not know that we were blind, bound and we did
not know that we were bound, and led by the
devil and we did not know that he was a-leading
us in the lost depths of poverty, and we did not
know that we were poor and miserable, and we
did not know that we were strangers and for-
eigners, and we did not even know that, and
while we were in that awful condition God, in
His goodness and mercy and love, provided for
us abundance of mercy and then turned around
and provided for us abundance of pardon.   So
we are agreed, so far, that the first two things
that we need are mercy and pardon.

Well, now, what is the next thing that we
need?   Well I believe that you will agree with
me that the next thing is the grace of God.   First,
mercy; second, pardon; third, grace.   Now if
you will turn with me to Paul's letter to the
Romans and read 5: 17, you will have the text:
"For if by one man's offence death reigned by
one; much more they which receive abundance of
grace and of the gift of righteousness shall reign
in life by one, Jesus Christ."

Now the reader will notice that in the above
text we are to receive the abundance of grace,

and then after we receive the abundance of grace, we are to reign with Jesus Christ. The thought carries with it the idea of kingship, and that is the thought that is brought out in the Book of Revelation, 1 : 5, 6, where we read: "Unto Him that loved us, and washed us from our sins in His own blood, and hath made us kings and priests unto God." In the quotation from Romans we see that we are to reign with Christ when we receive the abundance of grace and the gift of righteousness. The main thought is that the child of God is a man delivered from the affairs of this old world, and man is to look after himself and reign over himself. A Christian that hangs around the tobacco stand, and the cold-drink stand, and the circus, and the theater, and picture-gallery shows, and trots at all hours of the night to the secret lodges, is not a free man at all; he is as much bound by the devil as any man on earth. If he was ever converted, he is now a backslider or awful cold, at the very best construction that you can put on him.

The lodgeism of the present day is anti-God, and anti-Christ, and anti-Holy Ghost, and anti-Bible, and anti-Christian, and is "heap much devil;" it is the devil's church, and he is boss and general superintendent of the whole affair. There is not a man in the world that is a great lodge man that is a great soul winner; there could not be such a thing in existence, they don't go together, for one is the work of God and the other the work of the devil. There are hundreds of thousands of good lodge men in the United States to-day who if they were to die would spend an awful eternity in Hell, and yet they are splendid lodge men. Just this morning a sinner told me that he would love to come out tonight and hear me preach, but he said at the same time that they had a man to take into their lodge that night, and that he was expected to be there and help with the work of the lodge. He is a hard sinner, but a splendid lodge man; as much lost as if he were already in the pit.

The text says that we are to reign with Christ; delivered from the world and the flesh and the devil, filled with all the fulness of God and walking the earth a king, without one of the devil's strings on you. Christ said that the devil "has come and has nothing in me." Now, reader, can we say that much? If we are truly reigning with Christ, we can, but if you are mixed up with the world until you look more like a sinner than you do like a Christian, you can't say it.

To show you what I mean by looking more like
a sinner than you do like a Christian, the other
day in one of the little towns up in the state
of Ohio one of the young ladies who belongs to
the First Methodist Church, and also sings in
the choir, went to a big ball, and the lights
were turned low, and the devil came in and this
young lady danced with the devil. God knows
and the devil knows that she is not reigning with
Christ, but she is a-running with the devil, and
yet she is called an American "Christian." But
Isaiah said, "Therefore hath Hell enlarged her-
self, to receive thee at thy coming." At the time
he wrote this awful statement he was writing to
the Israelites, who had backslidden and gone
away from God; their feet were a-running to
evil, and their hands were defiled with blood, and
their hearts were like a stone, not only hard
but dead and without hope. You can see at a
glance that they were not a-reigning with Christ,
but I do thank God that there is a class of people
in the world that is in deed and in truth reigning
with Christ, and I am in that crowd. While time
and eternity last, they are mine, and I would
rather run with the Holiness crowd than to own
a world and be out of this blessed army and this
blessed fellowship; they just suit me, and when

anybody mistreats one of them I would rather
it was me than anybody else on the face of the
earth. With their mistakes and blunders (and
some of them have even fallen into awful sins,
not one of them were excused for it, although the
great crowd can't help what a few might do),
but taken as a whole, they are the cleanest set of
people in the known world, and they are the crowd
that is a reigning with the blessed Christ and
walking this old earth as kings.

Well, we are now ready to take the next step
as we climb up Jacob's ladder. The question
naturally arises in your mind, What is the next
thing that we need? Well I will take the ground
that it is the blessed Holy Ghost, and now if
you will turn to Paul's letter to Titus and read
3: 5, 6, you will have the text. Notice what he
says: "Not by works of righteousness which we
have done, but according to His mercy He saved
us, by the washing of regeneration, and renew-
ing of the Holy Ghost; which He shed on us
abundantly, through Jesus Christ our Savior."

Here the reader will see at a glance that the
thing that we are to receive the abundance of in
the above text is the Holy Ghost, and our hope
of success in this world is hung on the above
text, and our hope of Heaven is seen in the above

text, and the hope of the Church is seen in the above text, and even the world itself is dependent on the above text, for if the Church fails to secure the abundance of the Holy Ghost, she will have no power to convict sinners, and if the sinner is never convicted, he will die in his sins and be lost forever and ever, and the Church will be to blame, for God has provided abundance of the Holy Ghost for all His children, and if we fail to get it, we will fail to reach the sinner, and if we fail to reach the sinner, he will be lost, and God will require his blood at our hands at the great Judgment Day. So in the above text we see that we are to be regenerated, and then, in addition to that, we are to receive abundance of the Holy Ghost, and we all know that an abundance of anything don't mean meager supply or short rations, but it means a great quantity of the thing, all that you can use up and a big supply left over for the other fellow. Now that is just what God meant when He said that He was able to "make all grace abound toward you, that ye always having all sufficiency in all things might abound to every good work."

The great bulk of the Church to-day is living on half-rations spiritually, and, as far as we can see, they are buying their spiritual groceries on credit, and they are several months behind with their bill; and they are buying their spiritual clothes on the installment plan, and they are paying a little on them each month; and spiritually they are living in a little rented cabin, and are several months behind with their house-rent. They are serving the Lord in their poor, weak way, and they claim to be nothing more nor less than poor, weak worms of the dust, and when they would do good evil is always present with them.   They have found that Jordan is a mighty hard road to travel, and they have many ups and downs in life, but they want you to pray for them that they may hold out to the end.

I am ready to confess that they really do need our prayers, and we must pray for them, and love them, and point them to the Lamb of God that taketh away the sin of the world.   He is just a-waiting to give them abundance of the blessed Holy Ghost, but they haven't received Him yet, and the probability is that their pastor has been a-telling them for several months that they were as good as God ever expected to make them in this world, and that after death God can do great things for them.   We know that such things are going on all the time, and as we have the light and they haven't we must be as patient with them as the Lord has been with us, and we must bear with them long and be kind and gentle with them, for they are to be the next crop of Holiness people in this great country of ours. We must shout it loud and long, keep everlastingly at it and never let up, and let them know that the old Book said that God is able to make all grace abound, and then said that we were to receive an abundance of the Holy Ghost. Some of us well remember how hard it was for us to go into the fountain, and never stop until we were made whole, and cleaned up, and cleaned out, and filled up, and sent out, and charged and surcharged with compound lightning from the batteries of the skies, and made a holy terror to the devil.

Now we have seen that the first thing we needed was the mercy of God, and that the second thing that we needed was the pardon of our sins, and that the third thing that we needed was the grace of God, and that the fourth thing that we needed was the Holy Ghost, and now we are ready to see what the fifth thing is that we need. I will say that it is life, and then the abundant life, and for proof of this turn with me to St. John's Gospel and read chapter 10, verse 10, and you will have the words of the Master. They were these: "I am come that they might have life, and that they might have it more abundantly."

Now, reader, you will see from this text that we can have life, and that we can have it more abundantly. There is the second blessing, "properly so called," as John Wesley used to say when he was a-stirring the world by preaching the doctrine of holiness as a definite second work of grace. When John Wesley preached holiness, he could preach to five thousand people at five o'clock in the morning, and when the followers of John Wesley fight holiness, they can preach to fifty people at eleven o'clock in the day. See the difference? There is not a man in the United States that will get up at five o'clock in the morning to see a man smoke and hear him fight holiness. Well, John Wesley believed in holiness, and was afraid of worldliness, but the average Methodist preacher of to-day is afraid of holiness and loves worldliness. In proof of this statement, watch one of them go down the streets of the city at a late hour of the night, with a great gang of sinners on their way to the secret lodge-room where, in perfect alliance, he shakes their hands, gives them the grip or the handshake and the password, and becomes a partaker of their deeds. It makes the Son of God sick at His heart as that traitor stays out till one and two o'clock in the morning with a crowd just like Judas ran with. I don't wonder that they hate holiness. Look at him now with a rope on his neck, as he is now led by a band of sinners. Does he look like a servant of the lowly Nazarene? Listen to Paul, he says, "Be ye not unequally yoked together with unbelievers," and "What agreement has the temple of God with idols?" and, "What concord hath Christ with Belial? or what part hath he that believeth with an infidel? and what communion hath light with darkness?"

The text said that we are to have the abundance of life, and there is but one way to reason on this Scripture; be reasonable and scriptural, and I will give it to you right now. "I am come that they might have life, and that they might have it more abundantly," were the words of Jesus. He meant this; when He converts a sinner, He gives him life, and when He sanctifies a believer, He gives him the abundant life. He means this also; when He converts a sinner, He gives him love, and when He sanctifies a believer, He makes him perfect in love. He means this also; when He converts a sinner, He gives him joy, and when He sanctifies a believer, He gives him the fulness of joy. He means this also; when he converts a sinner, He gives him the witness of the Spirit that his sins are forgiven, and when He sanctifies a believer, He gives him the baptism with the Holy Ghost and fire and he knows that he is sanctified wholly. And He means this also; when he converts a sinner, He takes him out of this world, and when He sanctifies a believer, He takes the world out of him. He means this also; when He converts a sinner, He makes him a babe in Christ, and when He sanctifies a believer, He makes him a soldier of the cross. He means this also; that when He converts a sinner, he is at peace with God, and that when He sanctifies a believer, He gives him the peace of God that passeth all understanding. He means this also; that when He converts a sinner, he is made a conqueror, and when He sanctifies a believer, He makes him more than conqueror, through the blood of the everlasting covenant that was shed on Calvary for this lost world. Well, Amen!

Dear reader, we now come to the next round in the ladder. Will you turn with me to the 36th Psalm and read the seventh and eight verses? "How excellent is Thy lovingkindness, O God! therefore the children of men put their trust under the shadow of Thy wings. They shall be abundantly satisfied with the fatness of Thy house; and Thou shalt make them drink of the river of Thy pleasures." Now, reader, here are four facts stated that are enough to satisfy the most skeptical mind in the land. In the first place, we are to dwell under the wings of the Almighty; and in the second place, we are to have an abundance of satisfaction; and in the third place, we are to dwell in a house of fat things; and in the fourth place, we are to drink out of a river of pleasure. But that thought of abundance of satisfaction is the one that catches my eye. Just think of how little satisfaction the poor sinner has in this world; he carries first, a guilty conscience; second, a load of condemnation; third, a dread of death; fourth, a dread of the Judgment Day, and all of these monsters are on his track by day and by night. And he drinks to drown his troubles, and smokes to drown his troubles, when, if he was beautifully saved and sweetly sanctified, and if he could say, "I am abiding under the wings of the Almighty, and I am enjoying an abundance of satisfaction, and I am dwelling in a house of fat things, and I am drinking out of a river of pleasure," he would get more out of his life in

a single day than he has in all the days of his
life put together.   But the devil tells him that
the Lord is a hard master.   How strange it all
seems to a saved man!   Finally, as we go to
prayer-meeting some beautiful night, we hear
the crack of a revolver, and we are told the next
morning that some fellow gave up in despair and
took his own life, and the devil will laugh in the
face of the poor, lost soul as he plunges into an
awful Hell, and before night the devil has some
other poor boy to take the place of this victim
that went to Hell last night, and he knows that
in less than five years he will have this boy in
the same Hell that he put the other fellow in.
Well, the Bible says of the devil that he is a
deceiver. and if it was not true of him, he could
not do the things that he is a-doing.   He is a
mighty devil, but I do thank God that our Christ
is almighty, and that He is able to keep "that
which we have committed to Him against that
day."   We are to abide under His wings all the
days of our lives.

I have often thought that one of the most
touching incidents in the life of the Son of God
was when He saw the city of Jerusalem under
the dominion of the devil.   It broke His precious
heart, and He said, "O Jerusalem, Jerusalem,

thou that killest the prophets, and stonest them which are sent unto thee, how often would I have gathered thy children together, even as a hen gathereth her chickens under her wings, and ye would not! Behold, your house is left unto you desolate." He might have been at the home of a friend in the edge of the city and as the old mother hen saw the hawk in the skies and gave a squall and a cluck, and all the little chicks ran under her wings, He at the time looked out over the city and saw its awful doom a-coming, and He saw that there was no hope in the world for the city; and we read that He wept over the city. (See Luke 19: 41.)

But when we think of what He has provided for them that love Him and serve Him and honor Him, it is just simply grand. And think of how secure we are. What harm can come to a fellow if he is under the wings of the Almighty? See what joy comes to a man with an abundance of satisfaction; see what comfort comes to a fellow when he is in a house of fat things; see the holy delight that will play up and down on the face of a fellow as he drinks out of a river of pleasure, and as he listens to the voice of his Father as He says, "Help yourself, children; there is plenty more, yes, an abundant supply; it's yours."

Well, our next round in this remarkable ladder is Jer. 33:6. We read: "I will bring it health and cure, and I will cure them, and will reveal unto them the abundance of peace and truth."

Here the Lord tells us that He will reveal unto us the abundance of peace and truth. He don't say that we will grow very wise, and will make a very great discovery, and that we will find out the thing ourselves, but He tells us that He will reveal this thing unto us. So you see at a glance that it is not a discovery, but a revelation. It was revealed to us by the Almighty Himself, and for our good and for His own glory. We had no claims on the Lord at all; we were traitors to His kingdom and rebels in His government, but, in the face of it all, God loved us, bought us with the blood of His Son, and restored us back to His favor, and then made to us this great revelation, the revelation of peace and truth, which are two of the finest graces that go in to make up the life of a Christian.

There is much said about peace in the Bible. We read in Paul's letter to the Philippians (4:6), that "the peace of God that passeth all understanding shall keep our hearts and minds through

Christ Jesus." In Isa. 26: 3, we read, "Thou wilt
keep him in perfect peace, whose mind is stayed
on Thee: because he trusteth in Thee." And
again in Ps. 119: 165: "Great peace have they
which love Thy law: and nothing shall offend
them." There is a peace that nothing can offend;
that is worth paying the tax on, and you know
it as well as I do.

Again, Christ said, in John 8: 32 and 36:
"And ye shall know the truth, and the truth
shall make you free. . . . If the Son therefore,
shall make you free, ye shall be free indeed."
But He said it was all brought about by you
knowing the truth. When we reach the fourteenth
chapter of St. John's Gospel, Christ said, "I am
the way, and the truth, and the life," and in the
seventeenth chapter, He said to His Father,
"Sanctify them through Thy truth: Thy word is
truth."

It means much to have it revealed to us. It
was a wonderful revelation from God to man,
and He said, "I will bring it health and cure,
and I will cure them, and will reveal unto them
the abundance of peace and truth." That is,
He will cleanse the soul from all sin, and make
it healthy and strong, and will then make this

great revelation of peace and truth to the sanctified soul.

Well, now we have come to the next round in the ladder. We next notice (in the third chapter of Paul's letter to the Ephesians) that we are to have abundance of love. Notice chapter 3: 14-21: "For this cause I bow my knees unto the Father of our Lord Jesus Christ, of whom the whole family in Heaven and earth is named, that He would grant you, according to the riches of His glory, to be strengthened with might by His Spirit in the inner man; that Christ may dwell in your hearts by faith; that ye, being rooted and grounded in love, may be able to comprehend with all saints, what is the breadth, and length, and depth, and height, and to know the love of Christ, which passeth knowledge, that ye might be filled with all the fulness of God. Now unto Him that is able to do exceeding abundantly above all that we ask or think, according to the power that worketh in us, unto Him be glory in the church by Christ Jesus, throughout all ages, world without end. Amen."

The reader will notice that the apostle leads up to the thought of the abundance of the love of God. There is no way to explain the above Scripture and improve on it, for it is so full and

rich and sweet and full of juice and Heaven that
it would detract from it to try to explain it.   It
is better in Paul's handwriting than it would be
in mine; He said that he had been caught up
into the third heaven, and that he heard things
unlawful to utter down here.   Well, I say,
"Amen; so let it be, Lord!"

Well now, beloved, we have come to the last
round in the ladder.   We have seen the abundance of mercy, and the abundance of pardon,
and the abundance of grace, and the abundance
of the Holy Ghost, and the abundance of life,
and the abundance of satisfaction, and the abundance of peace, and the abundance of truth, and
the abundance of love, and now we come to the
last round in the ladder.   In 2 Pet. 1:11, we
read: "And so an entrance shall be ministered
unto you abundantly into the everlasting kingdom of our Lord and Savior Jesus Christ."   The
above text shows us that we are to have an abundant entrance into the everlasting kingdom of our
Lord and Savior Jesus Christ.

The Bible speaks of some people going to
Heaven and their works being burned up.   It
also speaks of a class of people who come rejoic-
ing a-bearing their sheaves with them, and now
in the above text we see somebody a-going up-

with an abundant entrance in. There is a sense in which the babe will be saved so as by fire; it hath no works to burn, but it will be saved only through the merits of the blood of Christ, and the idiot will be saved in the same way; they will both go in without a reward. Also the regenerated man that has lived long in the world with a Christian experience and yet has done nothing to help save the world; he has been regenerated and has not lost it, but he has never been wholly sanctified, so he will come to die and through the merits of Christ he will be cleansed and taken into Heaven, but he has done nothing, and his works are burned. The Bible says that he will suffer loss, but he himself will be saved, yet so as by fire. See 1. Cor. 3: 13-15, and you will have the key to the man that was saved so as by fire and his works were burned up. He will not have an abundant entrance into the everlasting kingdom, and, although he may be a fifty-year-old man, he will go into Heaven as completely without a reward as a baby or as an idiot. You see that his works were burned, and therefore it is impossible for him to have a reward.

Well now, in the outset I told you that God had everything in the world for you that you needed to make you pure and holy and kind and

loving and Christlike and gentle and good, and
if you will look at the Bible, you will see that I
have proven it all to you, and more, too. Just
look up the scriptural quotations and they will
satisfy the most skeptical man in the country.
There is no use now in living on half rations;
the table is set, and the bell is a-ringing, and the
table is a-groaning under its burdens of good
things. The invitation is to all: "Ho, every one
that thirsteth, come ye to the waters, and he that
hath no money; come ye, buy and eat," and let
your soul delight itself in fatness. Now, beloved, don't you stop until you know that you will
have an abundant entrance into the everlasting
kingdom of our Lord Jesus Christ. Amen and
Amen!

CHAPTER III.

THE TWO WORKS OF GRACE.

Dear reader, I want to talk to you about the two works of grace as we find them in the blessed old Book. Our text is found in St. Mark's Gospel, 8: 22-25: "And He cometh to Bethsaida; and they bring a blind man unto Him, and besought Him to touch him. And He took the blind man by the hand, and led him out of the town; and when He had spit on his eyes, and put His hands upon him, He asked him if he saw ought. And he looked up, and said, I see men as trees, walking. After that He put His hands again upon his eyes, and made him look up: and he was restored, and saw every man clearly."

Now, reader, here is a man that was born blind, and he stands as a representative of the unregenerated sinner. This man was physically blind, and the unregenerated sinner is spiritually blind; one was without physical light and the other is without spiritual light, but while this man was groping in his awful darkness, the blessed Christ paid a visit to his town, and that

was his opportunity. There is not a sinner to
be found in our land but who has rejected the
call of the Master to come to Him and get his
eyes opened and let the sunshine of Heaven
burst into his soul. There is one thing about
this blind man that is interesting to me; it is
this, he was ready and he was willing to be led
by the Master. And so we read that Christ took
him by the hand and led him out of the town.
There is not a sinner in the United States but the
blessed Christ would take him by the hand and
lead him out of a life of sin and sorrow and darkness and death and Hell if he would be led. We
read that one day the blessed Son of God said
to certain people, "But ye would not," and it is
the same to-day. Just listen to Him: "How
often would I have gathered ye together as a hen
gathereth her chickens under her wing, but ye
would not." Now listen again, "Therefore your
house is left unto you desolate," and from that
day Jerusalem was doomed, and she went down
with a mighty crash.

Now the next thought in the text that I want
you to notice is that the blind man was touched
twice. When the Lord touched him once he
saw men as trees a-walking. How natural that
is; as we look around us, we see the same sight

to-day. The unsanctified man to-day takes the place of that blind man when he had been touched once. The man had vision, but it was not clear; he saw men a-walking, but he saw them as trees a-walking. You notice he had to have the second touch to enable him to see all men clearly. Now the reader will notice these facts; the sinner don't see at all, he is blind, but the regenerated man can see, but he can't see clearly, he sees men as trees a-walking, but the wholly sanctified man has had the second touch and he can see clearly, his vision is as clear as the noonday sun, and he no longer sees men as trees a-walking.

When you get wholly sanctified, all men become the same size to you; you love men and honor men, but you worship God, and Him only. I have seen a pastor that weighed not less than 175 pounds stand before a presiding elder, and the elder would command him not to allow any Holiness preacher to preach in his church, or to preach on his territory, and the preacher would stand there and tremble in the presence of the elder just like a slave in the presence of his master. The pastor saw the elder as a tree a-walking, he never saw him as his equal and a brother beloved, he saw him as a boss and a ruler and a driver of mankind, a sort of a God-man. Now that is what the Book means by seeing men as trees a-walking, but I do thank God that this man got the second touch, and after he got it he saw every man clearly. Now I am going to make this challenge, that no man that ever reads this book has ever seen a man in anybody's church, I don't care how well he was educated, who, if he has never been sanctified, can write clearly on the doctrine of sanctification. You may take the most brilliant men and the best writers in the United States and let them undertake to write on the doctrine and right then and there they will run muddy. I have seen men that could take up the doctrine of regeneration, or justification, or the witness of the Spirit, or adoption, or repentance, or confession, and they could write on those subjects and make them as clear as a bell, but let the same man undertake to advance and undertake to tell you something of the deeper, richer experience of sanctification, and right there he runs muddy, and maybe in one discourse he will give you two or three different theories of the experience, and leave you completely in the wilderness without chart or compass, and maybe before he gets through, go so far as to tell you that there is no such experience. Well now, we would ask, What is the matter with that great, brilliant man?

Well, beloved, here is his trouble, he has only been touched once, and he thinks that he knows it all, and yet it is perfectly plain to the sanctified Christian that he is not a wholly sanctified man, and it is also plain that the man has never had the second touch, for he don't see clearly, his vision is not good. He can't see well enough to see that it is a sin to use tobacco; with one touch on his spiritual eyes, he sees a pound of satisfaction in one-half a pound of "Star Navy," but if he had the second touch, he would wash out his mouth, and would be ashamed to let the sinners know that he was ever so nasty and vile and filthy. And again, with one touch on his spiritual eyes, he can see much more in the square and compass and the latter "G" and the chain link than he can in the beautiful life of Christian perfection. Now the reason is just simply this, he hasn't had the second touch; he now sees men as trees a-walking, and to him the biggest thing in the universe is not Halley's comet, that has tied his tail five hundred thousand times around the earth, but the biggest thing is to be bishop in his church and rule men with a rod of iron, and to take a good, faithful pastor, who preaches scriptural holiness, and move him to the backwoods, and put a little tobacco-soaked, lodge trotter in his place. Don't that look like he needed a second touch?

My Father knows to-day, while I write these words, that I would rather be a second-blessing Holiness preacher than to own all the land on the face of the earth. No man living has a job that I want, for I have one that almost tickles me to death. Glory to God!

I believe that the Lord touched that man twice in order to teach us this beautiful lesson. There are two works of grace as clear as Halley's comet and you can see her if you look up, for she is there in full blaze, and her glory is a-swinging around this old world now. Hallelujah! that is just a little bit of our heavenly Father's fireworks, and it beats what Washington got up when Taft was innaugurated. That was as a thing of nothing, but watch that great old comet as she sweeps around this world and laps her tail across the face of our little earth a thousand times and laughs at us little fellows down here, but we will inform that great old comet some of these days that God is our Father, and that the comet is only one of the toys that our God made for His children to play with. And yet some little fellow will persist in teaching that God can't sanctify a man and keep him down in this country. Well,

when our Christ went back to the right hand of
the Father, He said that all power was given
unto Him in Heaven and in earth, and, thank
God! if our Christ has all power in Heaven and
in earth, that is all that concerns a man on the
road to Heaven, for he is not going to the other
country nohow. I live here now, and I am to
live in Heaven hereafter, and I am not going to
the other place. And I say, "Bless God, don't
you know you have nothing to fear, still believing
in holiness as a second work of grace, and preaching it as straight as a gun barrel, and so hot if
you sit down on it it will burn a blister on you?"
And it is up to the straight Holiness people of
America to live the life and preach the doctrine
in spite of all the fads and fakers of the country.

Well, now, beloved, we want to give you a
few more Scriptures on the two works of grace.
Now turn to 2 Pet. 3: 9, and read: "The Lord is
not slack concerning His promise, as some men
count slackness; but is longsuffering to us-ward,
not willing that any should perish, but that all
should come to repentance."

Here the reader will see that God, in His divine providence, provided repentance for the sinner and placed it in His will for him, and men or
devils can't keep a fellow out of the blessing that

comes to a man when he truly repents. There
is much said in the Bible on the subject of repentance, for it is the gateway into the Christian
life. No man can be a Christian that does not
repent of his sins, and then confess his sins, and
then forsake his sins, and then believe on the
Lord Jesus Christ. Therefore we see that the
doctrine of repentance can't be preached too
strongly or too often or too straight, for it is the
groundwork of every other step in the divine life.
If a man falls down on the doctrine of repentance,
he falls down on every other dictrine, and every
honest man to-day in the pulpits of the land will
bear me out in this statement, that the hardest
man to reach to-day is the unsaved man in the
church. Why is that? Well, it is because he
joined the church without ever repenting of his
sins, and he has built up a church membership
around himself, and when you go into his church
and preach to the sinners, he says, "Well, that
don't mean me, for I am a church-member," and
then you preach on the doctrine of scriptural holiness, and he sits back and says, "I feel no need of
that experience." Well, why don't he feel the need
of it? Just simply because a dead man don't
feel.

Now how are you to reach him? The best

way is to get him saved before he is ever taken
into the church, and then if he does backslide, as
men do sometime, he will always know that at
one time he was a soundly converted man, and
when you begin to preach to a backslider he
says, "Well, that is so, for I had that once." And
so you see it is easier to reach a backslider in the
church than it is to reach the man who has never
been converted.

Well now, we will turn to the next Scripture
and see what we can find in the will of our
Father for us. We have found that He willed
us the blessed doctrine of repentance, but now
turn to 1 Thess. 4:3, and we read, "For this
is the will of God, even your sanctification." Now
the reader will notice that God willed that the
sinner repent, and now we read that God willed
that the believer be sanctified; if one is scriptural
the other is, and if one is binding the other is,
and if one means what it says the other does, and
so we will just believe them both, and then we
will be sure to be on the safe side. The sinner
ought to shout for the next ten thousand years
to think that God loved him well enough to will
him the doctrine of repentance, for if God had
not willed it to him, he never could have repented,
for we can't get anything from the Lord that He

did not will us. And the very fact that God willed it to us proves that we can get it, and the very fact that God wills the experience of sanctification to His children ought to make them shout for the next hundred years.

But, I am sorry to say, I have seen a great many church-members who, when they heard that God wanted to sanctify them and make them holy, it would make them mad, and they would raise a racket with the man that told them about it. How strange it seems! It looks like every child of God, as soon as he hears about his great privileges in the atonement of Christ, would shout for joy and never stop until he had gone down and sought and obtained the Pearl of greatest price which is nothing more nor less than a clean heart filled with the perfect love of God, sweetly kept by the power of God, led by His Spirit, guided by His eye, upheld by the right hand of His righteousness, and his life hid with Christ in God. And then he will know what it means to be kept in the hollow of His hand.

Well now, reader, we will take another step in the golden ladder that reaches to Heaven. We have seen the two touches for the blind man and the two wills of the Father, and now we will take up the two manifestations of the Son. We

read first in First John, 3: 5: "And ye know that
He was manifested to take away our sins, and in
Him is no sin." Now the reader will notice in
the above Scripture that the Son of God was man-
ifested to take away our sins, and we believe that
He can do it, and we believe that He has done it.
Glory to His dear name! We have the witness
to it to-day a-burning on the altar of our souls.

Now the above Scripture is fulfilled in the
heart of every regenerated child of God on the
face of the whole earth, of any faith or order,
for no man's sins are taken away until he is regenerated and born again, and then he is adopted
into the family of God, and his name is written
in the Lamb's book of life, and he is now passed
from death to life, and from bondage to freedom,
and from darkness to light. His sins have been
taken away, for Christ was manifested for that
very purpose, to take away our sins. That is the
least religion that a man can get to get any salvation at all. The man that gets less than the
new birth gets nothing.

Although the new birth is a very great work
of grace in the heart of man, we don't know the
extent of it, and neither do we know the power
of it, and I doubt very seriously if we ever will,
at least in this world, understand the new birth.

There may be depths and heights of it that we may study for thousands of years after we have arrived at the home of the soul. The saved man is continually praising and blessing God for the fact that he has been born again, and that Christ was manifested to take away our sins, and that He has done it, and we know it a little better than we know anything else, it is such a knowable thing, and such an enjoyable thing, and such a livable thing, but not explainable.

Well, now, beloved, we take the next round. We have just noticed that Christ was manifested to take away our sins, and now we turn to First John and read 3:8, and we have this beautiful statement, "For this purpose the Son of God was manifested, that He might destroy the works of the devil." Now here the reader will notice that Christ was manifested that He might destroy the works of the devil. Now that is a different thing from what we have just been discussing. First, He was manifested that He might take away our sins; and second, He was manifested that He might destroy the works of the devil.

Here the reader will see the two manifestations of the Son of God. Now the "works of the devil" is, without a doubt, the carnal mind in the human heart. We read that the thing in the heart must be destroyed, and we read again that the thing is to be mortified, and then we read again that the thing is to be crucified, and neither of the above terms is ever applied to the conversion of the sinner, but always carries the idea of the converted man getting rid of the "old man" (as he is called in a number of places). In one place we read of the "old man" and his deeds, which means the "old man" and his children, and some of his children are old enough to name and have been named. Just listen to the "old man" call his children to dinner: "Anger, pride, jealousy, malice, hatred, variance, emulation, strife, wrath, drunkenness, murder, lying, fearful deceit," and such like as we read in the old Book. Now these are just a few of the "old man's" children.

We have just read that Christ was manifested to destroy the works of the devil, and now, reader, I am ready to admit that it looks like if Christ could destroy the green-eyed monster that is the father of all the above children, that every Christian on earth ought to go down before God and get the blessing, and the sooner the better. Why not throw up both hands and surrender just now, let the "old man" die, let Jesus crucify the "old man," back up the hearse, haul off a

load of carnality, cleanse the temple, set up the
banner over the door, and let the world see as
you go by that you have on your banner "Holiness unto the Lord"? If Christ can destroy the
"old man" and won't do it, then He is to blame
and not us; and if He can destroy the "old man"
and we won't let Him do it, then we are to blame.

Well, now, reader, we want to take up the
next two links in the golden chain. We notice
now the two prayers of the blessed Son of God,
one for pardon and the other for purity. We
read in Luke 23: 34: "Father, forgive them, for
they know not what they do." Here is a prayer
that was offered by the blessed Son of God for
His murderers, and you notice how Jesus prayed
on that occasion. He said, "Father, forgive
them." He did not pray that these murderers
might be sanctified, but that they might be pardoned. Well, now, reader, if the sinner is converted and sanctified at the same time, and if the two
blessings are just simply one work of grace, why
didn't Jesus, in His prayer, say, "Father, sanctify
them"? But He did not say that; He said, "Father, forgive them," and to a thinking man there
is nothing in the Book as interesting as the prayers of the blessed Son of God. The groundwork
of the salvation of souls of men is seen in the pray-

er of the Lord Jesus when He said, "Father, forgive them." We don't know just how it would
have gone with us if the blessed Christ had not
have prayed for us, but, bless His dear name!
He prayed for us, and we know that the Father
hears the Son when He prays for us; in fact,
we hear Him say at the grave of Lazarus,
"Father, I thank Thee, that Thou always heareth
Me." So, if the Father always heareth the
prayer of the Son, and if the Son prayeth for
us, then that prayer will be heard, and we will
receive the thing that the Son prayed for. If it
was pardon, that is the thing that we will get,
and that is the thing that every sinner needs and
must have or he is a lost man, but, thank God!
there is a full pardon a-waiting for every poor,
guilty sinner on the face of the whole earth.
Glory to God! Amen!

Well, Amen! We are now ready to look at
the other prayer that was offered to the Father
for us by the Son. We read in John 17: 17, these
words: "Sanctify them through Thy truth; Thy
word is truth." Now, reader, put these two
prayers down side by side and see the two crowds
prayed for and then listen to the wording of
these two prayers. Notice, "Forgive them," and
notice again, "Sanctify them," and when He said,

"Forgive them," He was a-praying for His murderers, and when He said, "Sanctify them," He was a-praying for His preachers. Well, now, beloved, don't you know that a murderer and a preacher ought not to be the same man? See how plain the Master made it; no way there to misconstrue His meaning. He said when He prayed for the sinner, "Father, forgive them," and when He prayed for a preacher, He said, "Father, sanctify them," and that is the natural order. How natural it seems to get down at the altar of prayer, and there you will find every one that prays at all, a-praying just like the Master. People are generally honest when they get down to pray. They will kneel beside the penitent sinner, as he weeps over his sins, and they will pray with all of their strength for God to forgive that sinner; they never think of praying for God to sanctify him, for when it comes to the show down, there is no man that really believes that God can sanctify a sinner. We all feel like he must be pardoned first, and sanctified later. I have heard preachers say that they believed that they got it all at once, and then turn around and say that their church is not ready for sanctification and the second coming of our Lord. The devil has a way of making it easy on a fellow to always be a-getting the blessing in the way that they never get it. The devil has a way of saying, "Oh, yes, you got it all at once. Oh, yes, you are to grow into it. Oh, yes, you are to get that when you come to die, there is no use in troubling yourself about what you can't get till you die." And men will say, "Well, that is so, and so I won't bother myself with it now. Good-by." But there is a fact about the doctrine and experience of holiness that won't be dismissed, and you can never say good-by to scriptural holiness and claim to be on the road to Heaven, for holiness is on that road and will meet you at every turn of life, and look you in the face and say, "Well, what about it, old boy? Here I am again, a-looking you in the face," and it is up to you to go down and get the blessing or get off of the road, for you must meet it day by day all the days of your life, and to-day the Master says, "If ye hear My voice, harden not your heart, as in the days of provocation, when they tempted Me and tried Me, and saw My works for forty years in the wilderness."

Now we will take up the next step and climb one more round in Jacob's ladder. We next notice that the Holy Ghost witnesses to the works of grace, and we will read Rom. 8: 16: "The

Spirit Himself beareth witness with our spirit, that we are the children of God." Now, reader, we know that if God's Spirit does bear witness with our spirit that we are the children of God, it must take place when we are converted, for notice this fact, if you were converted and God's Spirit did not bear witness to it, that you would be converted and would not know it, and if you were converted and did not know it, you could lose it and not know that you lost it. But this is the real fact in the case; when you are converted, God's Spirit does, then and there, bear witness to your spirit that you are a child of God, and then if you lose the witness, you know it a little better than you know anything on earth, that the witness is gone. Don't you see that there is no joy or peace or comfort in a salvation that a man did not know that he had, and don't you see that a salvation that is knowable is bound to be a great comfort to the possessor?

And so we are thankful to know that there is a salvation that is the most knowable thing in all the world, and we read it again, "The Spirit Himself beareth witness with our spirit, that we are the children of God.".

I have heard of people that inherited a very large estate and did not know it, and lived and

died in poverty, and I will never quit thanking
my heavenly Father for the great plan of salvation, that a man can be a Christian and know it.

Well, we now take up the last step in the
golden ladder of full salvation. We now read
Heb. 10: 14-16: "For by one offering He hath
perfected for ever them that are sanctified,
whereof the Holy Ghost also is a witness to us,
for after that He had said before, This is the
covenant that I will make with them after those
days, saith the Lord, I will put My laws into
their hearts, and in their minds will I write
them."

Now, reader, you will see here the blessed
Holy Ghost witnesses to more than one work of
grace. He will bear witness with your spirit
that you are the child of God, and we know that
that takes place when you are converted, and we
also see that God's Spirit will bear witness with
your spirit when you are sanctified, that the good
work is done in you. Now these two Scriptures
make the plan of salvation as plain as it can be
made—pardon and purity, conversion and sanctification, the birth of the Spirit and the baptism
with the Spirit, peace and perfect peace, joy and
the fulness of joy, love and perfect love.

The reader will notice these facts stated in

the last quotation, "For by one offering He hath perfected for ever them that are sanctified, whereof the Holy Ghost is a witness to us." Here we are sanctified, and made perfect, and the Holy Ghost is a witness to us that the work is done, and we know that the Holy Ghost could not witness to it if it was not done, and the very fact that the Holy Ghost witnesses to us that it is done is the best proof on earth that the work is done. So there is no room for a fellow to go on and be in doubt about it. If he will pay the price, and say, "Yes" to the whole sweet will of God, the Lord, on His part, will deliver the goods and cleanse the temple, and take up His headquarters there, and you will be one of them that know it.

CHAPTER IV.

The Three Ways.

Dear reader, we want to talk to you about the three ways that are found in the old Book. Of these three ways everybody on earth is found in one or the other.

The text is in 1 Cor. 12: 31: "But covet earnestly the best gifts: and yet shew I unto you a more excellent way." This text teaches the two works of grace, and the fellow that denies the fact will have an awful hard time to keep his head out of the mud. To prove that, first think of the statement of the text: "And yet shew I unto you a more excellent way." First, if these Corinthian disciples or Christians, as they were at that time (and no sane man will deny it), if they were yet unregenerated sinners, then a sinner is in an excellent way, and the regenerated believer is in a more excellent way, for whatever they were, either sinners or Christians, they were in an excellent way. From the fact the apostle says, "And yet shew I unto you a more excellent way," the reader will admit that they were in an excellent way, or it would have been impossible for the apostle to have showed them a more excellent way.

The man that denies the second work of grace will have to take the ground that the sinner is in an excellent way, and that the regenerated Christian is in a more excellent way and where is there a man that can take the ground that the sinner is in an excellent way and maintain himself in the Scriptures? Don't you see it can't be done? And so we can take this one verse of Scripture and drive every man from the field that denies the two works of grace.

To understand the text, you have to explain it as we find it in its three-foldness. It teaches three ways perfectly plain; the sinner is in a way that is not excellent, the regenerated believer is in an excellent way, and the sanctified believer is in the more excellent way. In that way the text is plain and to take any other ground will land you in the mud, and bog you so deep that you never will get out.

And now the first thing, I want to show you the three ways in the Holy Scriptures. Let the reader now turn to Romans and read chapter 3: 10 to 20, and you will have in these ten verses

the life-sized photo of every unregenerated sinner in the world. If the reader will now turn
and read the third chapter of First Corinthians,
he will be perfectly satisfied that the Corinthians
were converted, and yet not sanctified, as he finds
them in this chapter, and then if you will turn
to the third chapter of Ephesians and read that,
you will find the sanctified believers. You will
find that these three chapters teach or bring out
the three ways, and make them perfectly plain
to anybody that will believe the Bible.

But now we want to make it just a little
plainer that the Book teaches the three ways.
We will first turn to Gen. 6: 5: "And God saw
that the wickedness of man was great in the
earth, and that every imagination of the thoughts
of his heart was only evil continually." Now the
reader will see that here is a man in a way not
excellent. When the great God says of him that
every imagination of his heart was only evil
continually (and the text says that God saw
that), it don't say that He heard that man was
in a bad condition and about to go on to the
breakers, it says that he had done gone and
struck the rocks and went down with a mighty
crash and an awful wail, and that every imagination was bad; not a few of the imaginations

were a little bit warped, but every one of the
thoughts of his heart was bad, and bad all the
time. He don't say a part of the time, but He
does say bad continually, all bad and no good;
apart from God, he is hopelessly lost.

Now this text is a life-sized photo of the sinner, and shows him to be in a way not excellent.
Now we will turn and look at a fellow in the
excellent way, and see the difference between the
two, and a man half blind can see it. We now
turn and read 2 Chron. 25: 2: "And he did that
which was right in the sight of the Lord, but
not with a perfect heart." Here the reader will
see the difference between the sinner and the
righteous. Every imagination of the thoughts
of the sinner was only evil and that continually,
but notice the righteous, he did the thing that
was right in the sight of the Lord, but not with
a perfect heart. There is the picture of the man
in the excellent way; he was a-doing the thing
that was right, and the sinner was a-doing the
thing that was wrong—see the difference between the two? Now the man in the excellent
way proves two things; first, he proves that he
is not a sinner, for he was a-doing the thing
that was right in the sight of the Lord, and second, he proves that he was not sanctified, for he

did not do the thing that he did do with a perfect heart. So we have located the sinner and the justified man, one in a way that is not excellent and the other in the excellent way.

Now we take the third step and show you the picture of the man in the more excellent way. We now turn to Deut. 30: 6: "And the Lord thy God will circumcise thine heart, and the heart of thy seed, to love the Lord thy God with all thine heart, and with all thy soul, that thou mayest live." Now here is the picture of the man in the more excellent way, or the sanctified man. The reader will now see the difference; the sinner had a wicked heart, and the justified man had a righteous heart, and the sanctified man has a circumcised heart. See how plain it is?— wicked, righteous, circumcised; there are the three conditions in this country, the sinner, the justified, and the wholly sanctified. No sane man can read these Scriptures and fail to see that there are three ways brought out in these three Bible quotations, and that is in perfect harmony with the life and experience of every true child of God, justified first, and sanctified second. The sinner is all bad, the justified is mixed, and the wholly sanctified is all good.

But I know some will rise up and say, "But

there are a great many nice sinners, and honest
sinners, and charitable sinners." Yes, but all
dead in trespasses and in sins, so says the old
Book, and who shall we believe, the Bible or you?
God knows men better than men know themselves, and His record is that every imagination
of the heart is bad. But as we want to give
the old Book a chance to testify as to what man
really is, we now turn and see another sinner
described by the prophet Jeremiah. See Jer. 17:
9: "The heart is deceitful above all things, and
desperately wicked: who can know it?" In the
first quotation, from Gen. 6: 5, we had a heart
that was wicked, and that continually, but here
in Jeremiah we have a heart that is deceitful
and desperately wicked.

Look at the three leading words in the above
quotation — deceitful, wicked, and desperate;
there is something that looks like depravity to
this writer. That don't look like the sinner did
not need anything but to go to the university
for a few years, and take a thorough course of
training, and come out from the university a
perfect gentleman. No, sir, the man in the above
text will never be a gentleman until he is born
again and created over again, for his heart is
deceitful above all things. Notice, it don't say

that his heart is deceitful above a few things, but above all things, and then, in addition to that, his heart is desperately wicked. If I know what the above words mean, this man is prepared to commit any crime in the wide, wide world; he would make a white-slave dealer, or a saloon-keeper, or a gambler, or a murderer, or a wife beater and a child starver, or a home wrecker and a heart breaker; put him down to do anything on the face of the earth and he is ready now and waiting for the job. Wicked, deceitful, desperate just mean that he is bound by the chains of the devil and is prepared to commit any crime in the known world.

And yet we are told by many that the human family is essentially all right, and that we don't need the Atonement, and that we don't need the regenerating grace of the Son of God, and we don't need a Savior, because there is nothing to be saved from. But Jeremiah and Moses did not so understand the human family.

We next notice again the second stage, and see the man in the excellent way. We all know that the man that we have just described is in the way not excellent, and now to bring him up into the excellent way you will see that it takes a new birth to change him. We look first

at Ezek: 36: 26: "A new heart also will I give
you, and a new spirit will I put within you: and
I will take away the stony heart out of your
flesh, and I will give you an heart of flesh."

Now, reader, draw the contrast between the last
two scriptural quotations.   Notice, Jeremiah saw
a heart that was deceitful above all things and
desperately wicked, and Ezekiel saw a new heart
and also this new heart had a new spirit within
it.   There are two ways so plain again that a
man that can keep out of the creek when it gets
up can see it.   So we see that there is nothing
that will reach the sinner's condition but the new
birth.   He must be born again, not baptised with
water: not join the church, or join the lodge,
or the Brotherhood, that is not what the prophet
meant by a new heart.   He meant that the man's
whole affection was changed, and his nature is
changed in such a marvelous way that the things
that he once loved he now hates, and the things
that he once hated he now loves, and we see at
a glance that he has been translated out of the
kingdom of darkness into the kingdom of the
Lord Jesus Christ.   As Christ said, he is now
born from above, and that makes him a new
creature or a new creation, and he is now a
son of God and his name is written in Heaven.

Dear reader, we now take the third step again that will bring the man up into the more excellent way. We read in 1 Thess. 3: 13: "To the end He may stablish your hearts unblameable in holiness before God, even our Father, at the coming of our Lord Jesus Christ with all His saints."

The reader will notice that in the above quotation the heart is to be stablished unblameable in holiness before God. Now look at the last three texts quoted; Jeremiah saw a wicked, deceitful heart and Ezekiel saw a new heart, but the apostle Paul saw an established heart in holiness. The new birth is never called the stablishing blessing. There is, to a greater or less extent, an up-and-down experience with the most of the Christians until they get sanctified wholly and stablished in the fulness of the blessing of the Gospel of Christ.

The Book says that the unsanctified Christian is not stablished. "Well," somebody may say, "where is such a text?" Well we will look at St. James 1: 8: "A double minded man is unstable in all his ways." Here is the picture right before our eyes, here is a man with two minds in him and he is said to be unestablished; he is unstable in all his ways. If that don't mean an up-and-down life, what would you call it?

We know that a sinner hasn't two minds in him,
he only has one, and that is the carnal mind,
he is carnal throughout his whole being; and a
wholly sanctified man hasn't got two minds in
him, he only has one, and that is the mind of
Christ, and he is spiritual throughout his whole
being.   So it drops back on to the regenerated
believer to have the two minds in him.   We know
that when he was born of the flesh he brought
into this world with him the carnal mind, and
then again, when he was regenerated he received
the mind of Christ, and he already had the carnal
mind, and you see at a glance that he had two
minds in him, therefore James called him a
double-minded man.

We will give the reader one more quotation
from St. James, for he is very clear on the doctrine of the regenerated man a-having the carnal mind in him.   In Jas. 4: 8, we read, "Draw
nigh to God, and He will draw nigh to you.
Cleanse your hands, ye sinners; and purify your
hearts, ye double minded."   The reader will notice that the apostle addressed two different
classes in the above text; first, the sinner, and
second, the double minded.   Notice again, the
sinner was commanded to cleanse his hands,
and the double minded was commanded to purify

his heart. There are the two works of grace as plain and as clear as they can be made, and yet some good folks tell us that they can't see it. Well, some of us can. We know that when the sinner cleanses his hands every sin that he has ever committed is washed away in the regenerating grace of God, and we know that when a double-minded man purifies his heart all the inbred depravity that caused him to commit the sin that had to be pardoned was cleansed away by the blood of the Lamb, for we read that Jesus suffered without the gate, that He might sanctify the people with His own blood. (See Heb. 13: 12.) The double-minded man is one of the "people," therefore he comes in under the provision that was made for the double minded, for we all remember with perfect delight the favorite text about all the real followers of Christ, John 3: 16: "For God so loved the world, that He gave His only begotten Son, that whosoever believeth in Him should not perish, but have everlasting life." We praise the Lord for the above beautiful text, but that text is no more true than this one. Now listen to Eph. 5: 25-27: "Husbands, love your wives, even as Christ also loved the Church, and gave Himself for it; that He might sanctify and cleanse it with the washing

of water by the Word, that He might present
it to Himself a glorious Church, not having spot,
or wrinkle, or any such thing; but that it should
be holy and without blemish."

The reader will notice that John 3: 16 is uni-
versally claimed for the sinner, and we say,
Amen! it belongs to him, and it also belongs to
us.   But in Ephesians the fifth chapter, where
we have just read three verses, is another blessing as clearly taught as the other, and in this
text we have the work of Christ for the Church.
The apostle emphatically says that He "loved the
Church, and gave Himself for it; that He might
sanctify and cleanse it," so we see that the Father
gave His Son for the world and the Son gave
Himself for the Church.

In John 3: 16 there is provision made for all
men from all sin, for there is included in John
3: 16 more than the new birth, for we read in
John 3: 3 that we must be born again or we
cannot see the kingdom of God, and we also
read, in Heb. 12: 14, "Without holiness no man
shall see the Lord." So John 3: 16 must provide
a full redemption for all of Adam's fallen race,
that is, pardon for the guilty and cleansing for
the justified believer. The Father knew that we
had to have both, and it really takes two works

of grace to make a complete salvation from all
sin.   The justified believer has not full redemption, and he is without it until he is cleansed from
all inbred depravity and filled with the Holy
Ghost that brings a power and a glory into his
life that the new birth did not give him, as every
sanctified soul will testify.   There is no other
way to understand the meaning of the apostle
James if we fail to see the two works of grace
in James 4: 8.

Well, Amen!   Thére are tens of thousands
on this side of the beautiful city to-day that can
testify to the beautiful experience of both pardon
and also purity, and millions have crossed over
and to-day they are in the city of light a-waiting
for their loved ones, but all that have ever gone
into that city have had both pardon and purity.

Again, we take up three more Scriptures that
teach the three ways, that is, the way that is
not excellent, and the excellent way, and the way
that is more excellent.   We turn now to Rom.
2: 5, and read, "But after thy hardness and impenitent heart treasurest up unto thyself wrath
against the day of wrath and revelation of the
righteous judgment of God."

Here the reader will see again a picture of
somebody that is still down in a way that is not

excellent. Notice, first the heart was hard, and second, impenitent, and third, treasuring up wrath against the day of wrath. You could not think of a more fearful statement than the one above.

We yet fail to understand all that God means by a hard heart. Notice, we first saw in Gen. 6: 5, a wicked heart, and then, in Jer. 17: 9, we saw a deceitful heart, and now here in Rom. 2: 5, we see a hard heart. Now if you will just stop and think for a moment, you will see the natural process that the heart goes through to reach the final climax; first, wicked; second, deceitful; third, hard and impenitent, and in the last stage of the hard heart the fellow was a-treasuring up wrath against the day of wrath. There is the last stage of sin and wickedness before the sinner drops into eternity's night—wicked, deceitful, hard, impenitent, treasuring up wrath.

All of the Scriptures that we have quoted to the sinner prove the one and same thing, that is, that the sinner is in a way not excellent, and is exposed to the wrath of a sin-avenging God every day that he lives in sin. He is at least liable to drop into outer darkness any moment without another warning, for he has been warned, and plead with, and wept over, and prayed for, lo!

these many years, but still he goeth as the ox to
the slaughter. It may be that he has often been
to church, and he might have been a member
in good standing, for King Solomon said that he
saw the wicked dead and buried coming from
the place of the holy.

We next turn and see the man in the excellent way. Again we read, in Rom. 10: 9, 10:
"If thou shalt confess with thy mouth the Lord
Jesus, and shalt believe in thine heart that God
hath raised Him from the dead, thou shalt be
saved. For with the heart man believeth unto
righteousness; and with the mouth confession is
made unto salvation."

Here the reader will see at a glance that this
man is not down in the way that is not excellent,
but that he has been brought up into the excellent way, and he is in possession of salvation.
First, he confessed with his mouth the Lord
Jesus; second, he believed in his heart that God
had raised him from the dead, he believed unto
righteousness (so he had faith, you see); third,
he made confession unto salvation. So we see
he had a believing heart, and the other fellow
had a hard heart; there is the difference in the
two, one was hard and impenitent, and the other

believed unto righteousness and made a confession with his mouth.

Notice the above once more. "If thou shalt confess with thy mouth the Lord Jesus, and shalt believe in thine heart that God hath raised Him from the dead, thou shalt be saved." We see that this man was a-living a life of righteousness, or, in other words, he was a righteous man, and a righteous man is in a fine condition to get the blessing of full salvation.

Well, now we turn to our last Scripture and bring the fellow up into the more excellent way for the third time, as we have already showed you two other Scriptures that brought him up into the more excellent way. We read in Acts 15: 8, 9: "And God, which knoweth the hearts, bare them witness, giving them the Holy Ghost, even as He did unto us; and put no difference between us and them, purifying their hearts by faith."

Here we have the purified heart, which is the highest state of grace in the known world. When the heart is purified, there is nothing bad left in it, it is all good, and no bad. Glory to God!

Now, reader, that you may see the nine quotations all put in one bundle, that you may see the three ways perfectly clear, just turn with me and

we will look at them. First, we had Gen. 6: 5, a
wicked heart; second, we had 2 Chron. 25: 2, a
righteous heart; third, we had Deut. 30: 6, a
circumcised heart—there were the first three.
Now we will look at the next three. First, we
had Jer. 17: 9, a deceitful heart; second, we had
Ezek. 36: 26, a new heart; third, we had 1 Thess.
3: 13, the established heart. And now we will
look at the last three. First, Rom. 2: 5 was the
hard heart; second, we had Rom. 10: 9, 10, the
believing heart, and third, we had Acts 15: 8, 9,
a purified heart.

Here we have brought you nine Scriptures
that teach the three ways. The first three each
time brought out the picture of the man in the
way not excellent, the second three brought out
the man in the excellent way, and the third three
brought out the picture of the man in the more
excellent way. You see sin, righteousness and
holiness, and to-day, my precious friend, you are
in one or the other of these three ways; you are
a sinner under the condemnation of God, or you
are a true, justified believer, or you are a wholly
sanctified believer. And to-day, I plead with
you, step out of a life of sin up into a life of
righteousness, and then step up into a life of holiness, and then step up into Heaven. What say

you? I want to meet everybody that reads these
words at the Marriage Supper of the Lamb.
Christ said, "Come, for all things are now ready,"
and He said, "The Spirit and the Bride say,
Come, and let him that heareth say, Come, and
whosoever will, let him take the water of life
freely."

CHAPTER V.

Dear reader, we want to talk to you about exploits, as we find in Dan. 11: 32. He said that "the people that do know their God shall be strong, and do exploits."

I wonder if you have ever done an exploit? If you never have, it would be royal fun to sit back and see you make your first attempt at such a thing. An exploit is doing something out of the ordinary, and the most of the religious folk of the country are just simply a-dying with respectability. As nice a thing, and as beautiful a thing, and even as useful a thing, as respectability is, a man may have enough of it to kill him. A man may draw himself back into his religious hull and be as dead to all spiritual life as a clam in his hull in the bottom of the ocean, and a good loud shout or amen would scare him out of his wits, and he would almost jump out of his hide. At a glance you can see that he is not the man described in Dan. 11: 32. Daniel

said that "they shall be strong, and do exploits."
Well, he is weak and he is not doing any exploits.
He says that "still water runs deep."   Well let's
see if that is so.   I know of a pond of water that
don't run at all, and it is full of tadpoles.   I wonder if that is him?   Now it seems to me that
if I were to take water to describe my experience,
I would want to take a beautiful mountain stream,
a-whirling and tumbling and splashing and sparkling down the mountain side, and when I struck
the valley I would want them to use me to irri-
gate the beautiful farms of alfalfa and oranges
and plums and apricots and grapes and all kinds
of fine fruits.   Never would I want to compare
my experience to still water.

Now we will look and see that God has had
a few people all along the ages that could do
exploits.   We read in Exodus, the third chapter,
that Moses led a flock of sheep to the backside
of the desert, and the angel of the Lord appeared
to him in a flame of fire, out of a burning bush,
and Moses turned aside to see the great sight,
and God spoke to him out of the bush, and said,
"Moses, Moses," and he said, "Here I am," and
the Lord said, "Take off the shoes from off thy
feet, for the ground on which thou standest is
holy ground," and Moses at once obeyed and

stood in the presence of the Lord barefooted. It
is a strange thing, and yet true; when people get
close to the Lord they always begin to take off
something. Just the other day at the altar a
man and his wife got so close to the Lord that
she took off two finger-rings, and the man took
off a pair of cuff-buttons and a lodge pin, and
handed them over the altar and said, "Take these
and do something with them, I can't wear them
any longer." We look again and we see Moses
on his way to Egypt, with nothing but a shepherd's crook in his hand, but he is not down there
long until we see him a-coming out with about
three million people, and he never fired a gun.
Now that is an exploit. Again, we see him at the
banks of the Red Sea, and he stretches out his
rod and the red waters divide, and he brings out
his people without the loss of a man. Now this
is another exploit. It is not hard to find exploits
if we look at the right man, but we might watch
some men all the days of our lives and never see
an exploit. Again we see the man Moses with
his host at a bitter well, and they cried for water,
and he cuts a limb off of a tree and throws it
into the well, and behold! we see sweet water in
abundance. That is another exploit. Again we
see him in the desert with his great family; they

are out of water again, and he takes the rod in his hand and smites the rock, and great quantities of fresh, sparkling water come flowing out of the rock. Now, reader, I submit that to you as an exploit; what do you say? I leave that to your judgment as an honest man. And if we take the last forty years of the life of Moses, we have nothing but one great exploit. Every word that he spoke, and every step that he took, and every thing that he did was nothing less than an exploit.

Again, we read in Judges, the third chapter, of an ox driver who met an army of Philistines, and at once the battle was pitched and the fighting began, and when the battle was over there were six hundred men dead on the battle-field, slain by Shamgar with an ox-goad. Now, reader, that was an exploit of the first magnitude. I can see that old Judean ox driver as he made his way across the Judean hills punching his oxen with his sharp stick, and when the battle opened he thought nothing of a gun or bow or sword, but his ox-goad was good enough for him, and sure enough it was God's opportunity to show Himself strong in behalf of those whose hearts are perfect towards Him. (2 Chron. 16: 9.)

Again we read in the seventh chapter of Judg-

es, that the Israelites were overcome by the Midianites, but God had raised up Gideon to deliver
Israel, and God sent him out one night to spy out
the camp of the Midianites, and God allowed him
to hear a dream. One of the Midianites dreamed
that he saw a cake of barley bread tumble into
the camp of the Midianites and smash up a tent
and lay it down, and he told his dream, and
another man was the interpreter, and he said
that it meant that God had delivered Midian into
the hands of Gideon. At once Gideon made ready
to go to battle, but he did not understand that
God would do the thing in a most wonderful way,
and in a new way, and in a way that had never
been heard of before in all the world's history.
Gideon had thirty-two thousand men, while the
Midianites were without number, but the Lord
said, "The army is too big, cut it down." How
strange that seems to us to-day when every nation
on earth is trying to raise a large army. God
said the way for Gideon to get rid of his men was
to put them to this test, "Let every man that is
afraid return to his home," and twenty-two thousand started for their homes, But God said,
"You have too many yet, cut it down smaller,"
and at the next thinning out he cut it down to
three hundred. Quite a drop, from thirty-two

thousand to three hundred, but such is the working of the Lord. And now the Lord said to
Gideon, "Take three hundred pitchers and put
lamps in them, and get you three hundred trump-
ets, and give each man a pitcher and a trumpet,
and divide up your men into three companies,
and get down among the Midianites, and at the
given signal break your pitchers and shout, 'The
sword of the Lord and of Gideon!' and let your
men do likewise." Then you see Gideon and his
three hundred braves with a pitcher and trumpet
each. Now they are all in the right position;
Gideon gives the signal and each man breaks his
pitcher, and his light flashes, and he shouts,
"The sword of the Lord and of Gideon!" and
goes to blowing his trumpet with all his might.
The Midianites awake out of their sleep, and hear
the awful racket, and see the lights, and they
think they are multiplied at least a million times,
and it looked like the whole earth was covered
with the Israelites. The scene is so awful that
the Midianites go into war with each other
and begin to slaughter each other until they kill
the whole army.

Talk about exploits, we have them here in
great quantities. It is simply marvelous what
the Lord can do; His ways are past finding

out, and He never works the same way twice. His methods of work on the battle-field are not employed by Him at all on the next battle-field. The Lord seems to have so many different ways to win battles that He don't have to use the same method but the one time, and then set it aside and take up something new and unheard of, something that nobody on earth would ever think of but just Himself. Well, Amen! that all makes me feel so good, for He is my Savior and my Father both, glory to His great name! He never gets short of ways and means; He has them on hand to spare. There is no telling what we would do if we would just let our Father furnish us with a few of His own ways that have never failed, to use in place of our ways that never did succeed.

Again we read in the fifteenth chapter of Judges of another exploit. This time we have before us a man by the name of Samson, and we read of his conflict with the Philistines. In one battle he slew a thousand of their mighty warriors with the jawbone of an ass. His testimony was, "Heaps upon heaps, with the jawbone of an ass have I slain a thousand men." His slaying of the lion, and the breaking of the new cords,

and the breaking of the new withes, and the running away with the loom a-hanging to his locks,
and the killing of the Philistines, all show that
God raised him up to do these exploits. These
and the burning of the enemy's cornfield by catching the foxes all show us that Samson was not
an ordinary man, but a man chosen of God to
do some very peculiar works, to do things that
looked to be unreasonable and almost uncalled for,
but back behind him was the great God. He
works in His own way, and He never consults
men to see what they think of His plans of work.
To-day this old world, religiously, is a-dying for
an exploit. Everything that is done nowadays
is very common and very ordinary; in fact, a
man don't have to go to church if he don't want
to, he can stay at home and read the program
and get all that anybody else will get; no exploits
on the program, it is all common and all human,
nobody there to jump a bench or shout and turn
a summersault or a handspring, and pray a hole
through the skies and let Heaven drop out, and
let the crowd get a regular washout and down-
pour of the glory of God, for we all know that
nothing like that is ever put on the program.
Programs must be carried out in an ordinary way,
and nothing is to take place, only such as can

be explained away, and it generally is necessary to explain for nothing ever happens, and the world wonders why, and they have to explain.

We next notice a remarkable incident recorded in First Samuel, the seventeenth chapter. It is of David the shepherd boy and Goliath of Gath—a stripling and a giant; one a fair representative of the devil and the other of the Lord; one with heavenly artillery and the other with a sling; one giving out cursing and the other a-blessing the Lord. Goliath defied the Lord and David defied the devil: the giant went in the strength of the devil and David went in the strength of the Lord. The giant represents the boastful devil, as we behold him at the present day, as he defied both God and man. We see the devil to-day a-doing the same thing, but one of these days we will see the real King of Israel ride down on His white horse, run the giant devil down, behead him, rob him of his power and glory and shut him up in Hell forever and ever.

If you want to see the real exploit in this incident, read the forty-ninth and fiftyeth verses. You will see a lad a-going to battle with a sling and five smooth stones that he picked up in the valley, and behold! you look the second time and yeu see him a-coming back with a giant's head and four rounds of ammunition left over. That is one of the greatest exploits yet performed by man. We read that David brought the head of the Philistine to Jerusalem, but he put his armor in his tent. David kept it as a kind of a reminder, a curio, to let the world see in after years what the Lord had done by his hand; the head of the Philistine and his armor were a testimony to the world that David prevailed over the giant and came off of battle-field more than a conqueror. When David started out to meet the giant, he was unknown, but when he came back with the head of Goliath, he was well known in three worlds; he stepped to the front at one leap and went down in the world's history as a mighty man of war. One exploit is enough to put a man at the forefront, so our great need is men who can do an exploit.

We next notice, in the third chapter of Daniel, the three holiness boys who were cast into the fiery furnace. Talk of epxloits! we have them here in abundance. A man who can walk in the fire and not even get the hair of his head singed, and come out and not have even the smell of fire on him, is an exploit within himself, and of course all he does is just simply tainted with exploits; he looks exploits, and he talks exploits, and his act ions are exploits, and if you keep company for a few days with such a man, you will be a-talking exploits yourself.

The king made a decree that everybody who did not bow down and worship his golden image should be cast into the burning, fiery furnace, but, thank the Lord! all the folks did not go to meeting that day, they were at better business, they were a-serving the Lord while the hypocrites were a-bowing down to gold. It has been said that gold is an idol and is worshipped in every nation without a single temple and without a single hypocrite. But that is not all fact, as we see here, for there were three men that did not bow down to the golden image, as they preferred to be true to God and face a burning, fiery furnace. And they did it, and in doing that thing they did another thing, they changed the decree of the king, and he at once called his law-making body together and sent out his decree all over the nations that the man or people or nation that said anything against the God of Shadrach, Meshach and Abed-nego, he was to be cut to pieces. It is strange, after all that the king had said, how quickly he changed his mind and also his decree. Well, he had run up against an exploit. What if he had come in contact with a crowd of card-

players and dancers and theater-goers, do you
suppose that he would have had to change his decree? Never in the world! But thank the Lord!
he had struck the real thing and no make-believe
about it, for they said to him, as big as he was,
"Be it known to thee, O king, that the God that
we serve will deliver us out of the burning, fiery
furnace, but if He don't, we won't serve your
gods nohow." Well, thank the Lord! here were
three men that had the real thing and no make-
believe about it; they did not fear the face of clay.

We next notice Daniel in the lions' den. (See
the sixth chapter of Daniel.) We see this man
tried before the devil, condemned and cast into the
den of lions for the awful crime of praying three
times a day with his face toward Jerusalem and
his windows open. What a peculiar man he must
have been. He could have saved himself all
that trouble by praying in his house with his windows closed, and the blinds down, and the doors
all shut, and praying in silence; then all would
have been done in decency and in order, and no
trouble in town, he would not have been called a
disturber of the peace of Zion. It looks like that
Daniel was a little contrary and just a little bit
heady. The idea of the governors and rulers and
judges in the whole realm coming and asking a

favor of Darius, and it was this: "O king, live forever. And now let the king make a decree, that if anybody in thy kingdom ask a petition for thirty days of any other God or man but thee, O king, that he shall be cast into the den of lions."

The scheme of those dirty rascals was so thin that it would not hold water. Oh, my, it was that loose, so much like some things that I have seen in Texas that a fellow would think they were twin brothers. Their plan is laid and all the papers signed up properly according to the laws of the Medes and Persians that alter not, and now they begin to watch and chuckle and whisper around, "We have got him in our trap, and he will go to the den of lions, and we will get rid of this holiness crank." And sure enough, he went into the dens of lions, but, thank the Lord! he came out, and at the next business session these holiness fighters went in to see about the lions, and they never came out. Do you see the difference between the two crowds? Well, that is the way it will be at the Judgment Day. Daniel's trip was an exploit; theirs, a smashup.

We next notice a very interesting exploit, and it was a very unusual one. We read in the twentieth chapter of Second Chronicles of the Moabites and the Ammonites a-going up against Judah and Jerusalem, and they were like the grasshoppers for multitude, and they overran the country, and were stubborn and fierce, and they defied the people of God and looked a good deal like the boastful devil that showed himself in Goliath of Gath the great Philistine. And Jehoshaphat was not able to meet this mighty army with swords and spears and bows, but he went to God by prayer and fasting, and the Lord showed him what to do. He had him to appoint singers to go out and sing the beauty of holiness, to praise the God of Israel and give Him glory. They started out with their banners a-flying in the air and on their banners it said, "Holiness unto the Lord," and as the music began to arise, and the shouts began to roll, when the Lord heard them, He put such a scare on the Moabites and the Ammonites that they went wild with excitement and went to slaughtering each other, and when the Israelites came out into the valley to see what was done, they found the valley full of dead men; they had slain each other, and there was nothing for Israel to do but shout and sing and gather up the spoils. How much like a saved man that is to-day! All we have to do is to give God the glory and He will clean up the devil's patch every time and put them to fighting each other.

I see an exploit there that is encouraging to me when the battle is hot and the enemy is strong. We are to testify to the beauty of holiness and praise the Lord, and the battle is won, and the victory is ours, and the glory is the Lord's. Well, Amen!

I think that I have showed you enough exploits to convince any skeptic in the land that there are plenty of exploits on record in the Word of God. Let us all say, "O Lord, help me to do exploits before I die. Amen!"

CHAPTER VI.

A Fixed Heart.

Dear reader, I want to talk to you about your heart. There is much said in the Bible concerning the human heart, but the text that I wish to talk on to-day is Ps. 57: 7: "My heart is fixed. O God, my heart is fixed: I will sing and give praise."

In the first place, there is nothing on earth that can bring as great joy to the human family as a fixed heart. Until a man's heart is fixed, he is never satisfied and he is never established, and he is never at his best for God, nor for himself, nor for his family, nor his church, nor his country. But the Psalmist said, " My heart is fixed, O God, my heart is fixed: I will sing and give praise."

The reader will notice that the Psalmist repeated his statement, or, in other words, his statement is doubled like so many Scriptures we find showing more than one work of grace. It is like Gen. 19: 17, where we have the two escapes, and it is like Isa. 62: 10, where we have the two

gates, and it is like the two touches for the blind
man, in St. Mark's Gospel, 8: 22-25, and scores
of others that we could point out if it was really
necessary. But as it is not we will proceed to tell
what we think of a fixed heart, and the conditions
of a fixed heart.

Now, if a man's heart is fixed, he ought to
have the manifestations of a fixed heart, and he
will have, and they are so clearly marked that it
will be no trouble to tell the man with the fixed
heart, wherever you meet him. As the Lord
showed them to me, I will show them to you.
There are seven manifestations of a fixed heart.
We notice in the first chapter of Ezekiel that he
had a wonderful vision; he saw a very peculiar
creature, and it had four faces, and the first face
was the face of a man. Now a man with a fixed
heart is a natural human being, and every man
on earth that hasn't had his heart fixed is abnormal and unnatural. As long as the carnal mind
is in the heart, there are manifestations of anger,
and jealousy, and pride, and a host of other
things, and the man is abnormal and unnatural.
In fact, he is not a natural human being until he
gets his heart fixed. Anger is not natural, it is
abnormal, it don't naturally belong to you and
you would be much better off without it. Pride

came in after the fall of man, therefore it don't
naturally belong to you, it is harmful and unchristlike, and you see at a glance that you would
be better off without it than with it. So the man's
face in the vision represents the natural human
being, and to be natural is one of the most beautiful graces that a man can be in possession of,
but no man is natural until he gets his heart
fixed, and no man's heart is fixed as long as the
carnal mind is in there, and any man with the
carnal mind in his heart is a dangerous man.

But notice again. The Psalmist said, "My
heart is fixed, O God, my heart is fixed: I will
sing and give praise." No man is in any condition to sing and give praise until he gets his
heart fixed. A mad man, or a proud man, or a
jealous man is in no condition to sing, the melody
of Heaven is not in the heart of an angry man,
and the songs of a proud woman are disgusting
to the public.

And so, after all, one of the most beautiful
graces I ever saw was the grace of naturalness.
Man, before the fall, was natural, but when sin
entered the heart, the man then and there became
unnatural and unchristlike and unfit for Heaven.
The sinner is out of harmony with God in every
sense of the word; the regenerated man is re-

stored in part, and the wholly sanctified man is restored completely, so far as cleanness is concerned. I don't know if we ever will be, in this world or in Heaven, what we would have been if we had never sinned, but we know that we can be cleaned up and cleaned out and kept in that condition while we are in this world, and that is the condition of a man with a fixed heart. A man with a fixed heart is as well prepared for the duties and the responsibilities of life as a man will ever be in this country, and if your heart is fixed it will keep perfect time with the great clock on the walls of Heaven, for you are natural.

Now we will take up the second condition of a fixed heart, or rather, the second manifestation of a fixed heart. The second face that Ezekiel saw was the face of a lion. Now, a man with a fixed heart is not only natural, but he is as bold as a lion; he neither fears men nor devils. He now has the courage of his conviction; he will wash out his mouth, and tear off his lodge pin, and vote the Prohibition ticket. Even if he knows that the man that he voted for would not be elected, he would rather vote for a clean Prohibitionist and get defeated in the election than to vote for a rumseller and elect him, and you would, too, if you are natural and bold.

One of the most beautiful graces that a man can be in possession of is the grace of boldness, and, brother, if you are a-going to succeed in this life, you will have to have a backbone as big as a sawlog, and ribs like a column of steel, and a Heavenborn conviction, and you will have to stand by your convictions at any cost. If the devil can whistle you off, and the mob can choke you off, you may just as well quit now, for you will never succeed in this world.

They tell me that when the lion was made the ingredient that is called fear was left out of his makeup. He is by no means the biggest thing in the woods, but men tell me, that are in a position to know, that when the lion shakes his shaggy mane, and his copper eyes begin to glitter, and he gives a few deep growls, every animal in the forest begins to scratch gravel and look for a hollow log. There is but one explanation to it and it is that he is a lion. Brother, when you meet him, it is just simply fight a lion or scratch gravel, and no man is bold as a lion with the carnal mind in him; it will have to come out before you will look this world in the face and stand square by the things of the Lord.

But somebody says, "Well now, Brother Robinson, I know a man that is no Christian at all,

and he would fight a dozen men with shotguns."
Well, brother, that is not boldness, that is the
devil in him, and the same man that will fight all
the men in the settlement when he is full of anger
is at the same time afraid to pray, and you can't
get him on his knees at all. He is, after all, a
cold-blooded coward, and afraid to go out of his
own home without a gun, and anybody can see
at a glance that he is altogether without the thing
that I am talking about. It takes no courage at
all to do wrong, but, beloved, it does take courage,
and a great deal of it, to do the right thing at all
times.

There are but few people on the whole earth
that have the courage of a lion when it comes to
the principle of the Lord Jesus Christ. Look at
the great pulpits and the great political parties
of our nation, and see them all quail before the
liquor and tobacco traffic and the white slave
traffic. A few bartenders and a few city harlots
can carry most any city election. Brother, I
tell you face to face, that the average man is altogether without the courage of his own convictions. They know just what ought to be done,
and they wish that it could be done, but they
themselves are afraid to speak up and let the
world know how they feel on the subject. The

great God of all the earth has given us the face
of a lion as a model to go by. Andrew Jackson
said, "Know that you are right, and then go
ahead." Well, Amen! so much for that.

O dear Lord, give us one of such men in
every pulpit, and one in every office, and we will
reform the United States in a few years. A man
with a fixed heart, and his path lit up with the
shining light of the Judgment Day, will know
his duty and perform it at any cost, in spite of
men or devils. Such a man will be a terror to
the devil, and a mystery to the folks, and misun-
derstood by plenty of good folks, and plenty of
good people with weak backs will even oppose him
and think him just a little overzealous. Where
is there a man but what knows that decency and
civic righteousness ought to be on the banner of
every city in the United States, and float in the
breezes, and let the passing world see the banner
of a nation that is built on righteousness, and
where is there a man but what knows that every
pulpit in the land ought to declare the whole counsel of God? But let some faithful officer of the law
begin to prosecute the criminals of the city, and
let some faithful pastor begin to cry out against
sin, and the bums and cutthroats and the gutter-
snipes and the city harlots and the backsliders

will raise an awful cry, and put up an awful howl, and two-thirds of the good people will turn their heels on the faithful officer and pastor, and fly for their lives, and often join the downtown crowd and vote to reinstate wrong and vote to defeat right. By their ballots they will put wrong on the throne and put right on the scaffold to be crucified, and then cuss hard times for the next four years.

Lord, make me as bold as a lion, and, if it is possible to do anything with me, let the world know that I am a second-blessing, Holiness man, and a Prohibitionist; that I believe in holiness in the pulpit, civic righteousness in the courthouse, and a family Bible on the center-table of every American home. A home with a deck of cards on the center-table and a keg of beer in the cellar will produce girls for the brothel and boys for the gutter, and bring the old gray hairs down to the grave in sorrow and shame and disgrace.

But there are so many that are afraid of popular opinion and of what somebody will say, that they tremble in the presence of clay—not Henry Clay, but the face of man. We must honor the man in that we respect all men in the Lord, but stand by the right at the cost of friends or anybody else that would come in between you and

God; God must be first or He will not be at all.
And, beloved, you will need a little courage to do
the whole will of the Lord, and to stand at your
post of duty as a good soldier of Jesus Christ.

Well now, reader, we have come to the third
manifestation of the fixed heart. The third face
that Ezekiel saw was the face of an ox. You
will notice that a man with a fixed heart was first,
natural; and second, bold; and, in the third place,
he will be as patient as an ox. Now while the
lion is the boldest thing in the world, he is without
patience, and if you fool with him, he will break
your neck in a minute, but the ox is not bold at
all, but he is the patientest thing that is known
to man. The lion takes it over everything for
boldness and the ox takes it over everything when
it comes to patience; each one has his beautiful
characteristic.

So if a man's heart is fixed, he will be first
natural, and then bold, and then patient. There
are few men that don't need more of the ox. A
patient man is a walking curiosity on the face of
the earth. The world has seen men without
patience until, to see one with it, they are surprised and wonder what is the matter with him;
they think he is too dead and stupid and lifeless
to raise a racket; they don't know it is patience

that he has, they think that he is too dull to protect himself when he is set aside and he goes on
and says nothing.

But, after all, the world is dying for enough
patience to enable them to live the Christ life.
The old Book says, "And He opened not His
mouth." Oh, beloved, if that could have been
said of us, what joy that would bring to our
hearts and lives, that he or she opened not his
mouth or her mouth, as the case might have been.
How quick we are to speak up, and how easy it
is to show a little impatience, and in a little act
lose a big blessing, and in a little impatience commit a big crime. How often it has been done by
you and this writer. Oh, beloved, are we like
the ox? I have seen the ox in the bog, loaded
down until he could not pull out, and he would
pull as long as he could stand, and when he could
pull no more he was as patient as if he had been
out on the good ground.

The ox represents patience and endurance.
We are to endure hardness as a good soldier of
Jesus Christ, and no man can endure hardness as
a good soldier until he gets his heart fixed, and
no man has his heart fixed until he is as patient
as the ox; or, in other words, the fixing of his
heart produces the patience of an ox. And now

he is natural and bold and patient—there are
three of the manifestations of the fixed heart.

I would suppose that there was no Christian
grace that would add more to the life of the average Christian than a good stock of patience, and
I think that the time has fully come for us to get
down on our knees and pray this kind of a prayer:
"O Lord, for the cause of my blessed Christ, and
for the great cause that I represent, give me
some more ox, give me ox, Lord; more ox, more
ox!"

It is said that the ox is patience personified,
and that the lion is boldness personified, and if
you are natural and then have the lion and the
ox both, you are just about a-flying. Now, old
boy, you don't have to look down your nose.
See that man out there, perfectly natural and
easy, tidy and neat, and adjusted to his situation, no friction, no hot-box, he is just natural,
that is all; aint he beautiful? See him when the
occasion demands it, he is as bold as a lion.
Don't you see something about him to attract
your attention? See him when everything goes
wrong and everything turns against him, he is
as patient as an ox and as calm as a May morning, and will shine like the dew on the red-top
clover. It is said of Stephen that his face did

shine like the face of an angel, but, oh, beloved, he was natural, and he was bold, as you know, and he was patient, and while the rocks whizzed, he said, "I see Jesus." But nobody thinks that the rest of the crowd saw Him, and, in fact, they know that they did not, but the patient Stephen, in the presence of grinning teeth and flying rocks, saw Him, and left his beautiful testimony on record. Oh, to be as patient as the ox! What would it mean?

Dear reader, we have now come to the fourth manifestation of the fixed heart. You will remember that the fourth face that Ezekiel saw was the face of an eagle. There are many things said in the Bible about the eagle. In Ex. 19: 4, we read: "Ye have seen what I did unto the Egyptians, and how I bare you on eagles' wings, and brought you unto Myself." Again, we read, in 2 Sam. 1: 23, that "Saul and Jonathan were swifter than eagles, they were stronger than lions." And again we read, in the Book of Job, 39: 27-29: "Doth the eagle mount up at thy command, and make her nest on high? She dwelleth and abideth on the rock, upon the crag of the rock, and the strong place. From thence she seeketh the prey, and her eyes behold afar off." Again we read, in Ps. 103: 5: "Who satisfieth thy mouth with good things; so that thy youth is renewed like the eagle's." And again we read, in Isa. 40: 31: "But they that wait upon the Lord shall renew their strength; they shall mount up with wings as eagles; they shall run, and not be weary; they shall walk and not faint."

Now there is no use in piling up more Scriptures. These will show you that there are many things said about the eagle in the Bible. The eagle is called the king of birds because he can cleave the blue as nothing else can do it. He never gets caught in a storm. When the black cloud begins to roll up, the eagle takes to his great wings, and sails above the clouds, and sails around in the blue sky, and mingles in the lovely sunshine, while a mile below him is an awful storm a-raging. The thunders roll, and the lightnings flash and leave death and destruction in their pathway, but the eagle don't even get his feathers ruffled, and it is all because he is above the storm-line.

And to-day, while tens of thousands of Christians are swept off of their feet by the awful storm of temptation of the devil, and carried down the awful swollen streams of worldliness, other Christians in the same community are kept sweetly in their souls, and it is because they are eagle-like; they have built their nest on the Rock of Ages, and set their nest on high. They have mounted up with the wings of an eagle and they are above the storms of the devil. And while some Christians are a-gritting their teeth and a-pulling their hair and a-having the most awful struggle of their lives, others in the same community did not know that there was a storm on at all and it was all news to them when they heard that an awful storm had been a-sweeping the country. Well, they are kept by the power of God through faith unto salvation, ready to be revealed in the last times.

You will notice that in Saul and Jonathan the eagle and the lion are combined, and so they are in all truly sanctified souls. A man with a fixed heart is as bold as a lion and as swift as the eagle.

Again, the eagle is a high-land bird, he is never caught down in the swamps, he lives on the mountain-top, where the sun is always bright and the air is always fresh. Job said that he could see afar off. Of course he can, and so can you, if you will get on the top of the mountain.

Again, it is said of the eagle that he is a very clean bird, that he never eats anything that he finds dead, he only eats what he picks up him-

self, and he always wants it fresh and warm.
When he gets hungry, he swoops down on an
English sparrow and takes him alive and eats
him warm and fresh.   Well, don't you remember
that the Lord said to the Israelites that when
they killed a lamb if it was too big for one family
they were to have their neighbors over to take
supper with them, and after they had all eaten
a-plenty, if there was any of the lamb left over,
they were to burn it with fire so that there would
be none of it left over?   This proves that the
Lord don't want us to live on cold hash.   Don't
you see that He wanted them to have a warm,
fresh meal every time?   Well, just so with our
religion, we are to have a fresh supply on hand
all the time, and we are not to live on what we
had yesterday; the Lord is able to furnish us with
all that we need.   Don't you see if He could furnish the sons of Jacob with a fresh lamb each
day, that He can furnish you with a fresh cup
of grace each day?

Again, it is said of eagles that they are very
strong and ferocious, and that they will fight
for their young till they die.   Don't you see
that if we were like the eagle we would be strong
in the Lord and in the power of His might, and
that we would put our arms of love and faith

around our family and fight for them till we die, and never give up the battle until we see our children saved in the ark of the everlasting covenant?

You see we are to mount up like the eagle, and we are to be swift like the eagle, and we are to build our nest on high like the eagle, and we are to live above the storms like the eagle, and our home is to be on the rock like the eagle, and we are to see afar off like the eagle, and we are to have warm, fresh meals like the eagle, and we are to protect our families like the eagle, and we are to live in the sunshine like the eagle, and we are to breathe the mountain air like the eagle, and we are to keep out of the swamps like the eagle.

Well, thank God there is plenty of room for you and the eagle both on the mountain-top! It is a large country up here, much larger than the average Christian supposes. They think, from what they can see down in the valley, that the country is very small on the top of the mountain, but when we finally get them to make just one trip to the top of the mountain, they see so much more country than they supposed was there that they are surprised beyond measure, and when they get to the top of the mountain and get one good look at the country, they see miles and miles of beautiful country that they did not know was in existence, and they look back at the little valley and it don't look bigger than a chicken-coop, and they are surprised that they could have stayed there so long.

Dear reader, we have now come to the fifth manifestation of the fixed heart. You will find it in Matt. 10: 16. We see that if a man's heart is really fixed, he will be as gentle as a lamb. We have seen him natural, bold, patient, swift, and now he is gentle. While the lion is the boldest thing in the universe, the ox the patientest thing on earth, and the eagle the swiftest thing on wings, the lamb is the gentlest thing on the face of the earth.

The lamb has many qualities that nothing else on earth is in possession of. He is gentle, he is charitable, he is unsuspicious, he never protects himself, and in these four particulars he is different from all other animals. It is the nature of the sheep to love to be taken care of by somebody else; he never thinks of providing for himself. The sheep will lay down in the fence corner and starve to death in sight of plenty, but not so with the goat. The old billy goat will climb the ladder, get into the barn loft, and help himself, while the sheep stays on the outside and starves to death.

And after all, how helpless are we! If our heavenly Father don't feed us, we will starve. You may take the richest country on earth, and if your heavenly Father don't supply you with seeds, you will starve to death. You can't raise one mouthfull of food without the aid of God.

And how beautiful is the spirit of a man that is gentle and dependent, and how disgusting is the spirit of a man that is full of pride and self-conceit.

The lamb loves to be led in and out to his pasture by somebody, and talked to and petted and fed and watered at the hand of somebody else, and if his shepherd is near him, he will lay down and rest and feel safe and protected from all harm. How much like the true child of God that is! Oh, beloved, how helpless we are and how dependent we are on the great God! Beloved, if you claim to be a Christian, let the world see that you are gentle.

Again, the lamb is charitable. The lamb will lay up on the bench and let you cut every thread of wool off of his back and never bleat, but how different it is with a goat! If you go to shear a goat, he will alarm the whole settlement,

and everybody in hearing will know that somebody is a-shearing a goat, and I fear that many
goats have joined the church, and are a-passing
off themselves for sheep. But let the pastor take
up a missionary collection, and you will hear the
bleating of the goat. The sheep gives up his
wool without a word, but the goat will raise
an awful racket if you go to take his hair. So
you see at a glance that, if a man's heart is fixed,
he is gentle and charitable.

But again, the lamb is not suspicious. I have
known the dogs or wolves to get into a flock
of sheep and kill the whole flock on a lot not
two hundred feet square, and if the sheep had
have been the least bit suspicious when the dog
caught the first one, the others could have fled
to the barn and have saved their lives, but they
won't do it, they will stand by and watch the
dog kill one and never try to escape, and not
even feel that they are in any danger. But how
different it is with the goat! If you climb the
pasture-fence the goat thinks that you are after
a fight, and at once he is making preparation for
a mighty hot fight. Now, beloved, there is the
difference between a Christian and a sinner.

And again, the sheep never protects himself;
anything else will fight till it dies, but not so

with the sheep. The sheep was never known to fight when he was caught by a dog or a wolf. They will humbly submit to their fate and lay down and die without a word of complaint.

And the sheep will go anywhere on earth that his shepherd will lead him. Beloved, if we would follow our Shepherd like the sheep wi'l follow his, there is no telling on earth what He would do for us. We would be fed, and clothed, and protected from all harm and danger, and goodness and mercy would follow us all the days of our lives. Well, Amen and Amen!

Dear reader, we have come to the sixth manifestation of the fixed heart. Christ said that you are to be as wise as the serpent. So you see that we are to be natural, and bold, and patient, and swift, and gentle, and wise. The lion is the boldest thing on earth, the ox is the patientest thing in the world, the eagle the swiftest thing on the wing, the lamb is the gentlest thing that is known to man, and the old serpent is the wisest thing that crawls on the dirt. And so our great need is wisdom. We are to know how to conduct ourselves at home or abroad. When something is to be done, we are to know how to do the thing, and when something is not to be done, we are not to do the thing.

Where there is good to be accomplished, we are
to push the battle and shine and shout; and
where there is evil, we are to touch not and taste
not and handle not.

One of the great needs of the religious worker
of to-day is spiritual wisdom.   It means so much
to know how to go back into a crowd of people
and speak to a man about his soul, and be able
to draw him instead of driving him.   It is a
sad mistake to go to talk to a man about his
soul and take your butcher-knife and steel rod
and your pitchfork along; that is, if you expect
to win him to the blessed Christ.   Notice, Christ
said to be as wise as the serpent.

The reader will see that if a Christian is
natural, and then bold, and then patient, and then
swift, and then gentle, and then wise, you will
see at a glance he is capable of doing untold
good.   And all of the above manifestations can
be had by men or women that never went to
school a day in their lives.   All of the above
gifts are sent down from above and not handed
out from the gray walls of the great universi-
ties of the land.   You will understand that a
good education is a great blessing to anybody
on earth, but, after all that can be said in its
favor, it is not spiritual gifts, for the most

learned of the land are the least spiritual, and seem to know the least about God and the workings of the Holy Ghost. The wisdom of man, at its best construction, is only human and not very far reaching. What one man of great learning gives out to to-day as a scientific fact will be disputed to-morrow by another man as wise as he is.

We read in Jas. 3: 17: "But the wisdom that is from above is first pure, then peaceable, gentle, and easy to be entreated, full of mercy and good fruits, without partiality, and without hypocrisy." Now this is the wisdom that a man has when his heart is fixed, and I don't wonder that the Psalmist said that he would sing and give praise, for when a man's heart is fixed he is then and there prepared to do anything that is lovely and beautiful, and singing and giving praise are among the lovely things of the life of the New Testament Christian.

Some good people get into all the trouble that is in the country, while others keep out of it all, and the difference is just this; one has spiritual wisdom and the other hasn't, one listens to the voice of the people and the other to the voice of God.

The reader will notice that James said "the

wisdom that cometh down from above." Now
James speaks of a "wisdom that descendeth not
from above, but is earthly, sensual, and devilish."
(Jas. 3:15.) So there are two kinds of wisdom, one from above and the other from the
earth, and the last smatters of the things of this
world. The devil seems to have his hand on
the wisdom of this world, and he is using it to
glorify himself with, and in that particular he
is showing himself to be the god of this world.
We must have the wisdom of a serpent to detect
him in his plans and schemes, and if we are
in possession of that wisdom that cometh down
from above, we will know him and understand
his workings, and by the grace of God and the
power of the blessed Holy Ghost we will be able
to meet him and defeat him, and come out victorious over the head of the enemy every time.
Well, Amen! Bless the Lord for this wonderful salvation!

Well, Amen! bless the Lord we are a-climb-
ing up Jacob's ladder. We have now come to
the seventh manifestation of the fixed heart, and
the last one is the most beautiful one of all the
different manifestations of the fixed heart. Now
listen to the words of the Master: "Be ye as
harmless as doves." I suppose that the dove is

the most beautiful in its life in the world. From wisdom that cometh down from above." Now the day that Noah put his hand out of the window of the ark and took in the dove with the olive leaf in her mouth, and from the day that Christ stood on the banks of the Jordan and the Holy Ghost came on Him like the white dove, and from the day that Christ said to the disciples to be as gentle as lambs, as wise as the serpent and as harmless as the dove, from that day till now men have taken off their hats to the dove. No harm in the dove at all; of course there would not be any, for Christ could not have said to a preacher to be as harmless as the dove if there had been any harm in the dove at all.

Again, it is said that when two doves mate they are mated forever; they were never known to have a family quarrel. We might learn a fine lesson there, and improve on the race of mankind by watching the birds.

Again, it is said that when they go to feed they feed side by side, as a general thing, and as they hunt for their feed they carry on the most lovely conversation between themselves that you ever heard. The most of the time while they hunt for their food they are only from six to ten inches away from each other, and every-

thing that the little male bird finds he makes his
little bride take it and eat it, and everything that
she finds she makes him eat it, and so they seem
to love each other with a perfect heart, and work
for each other's interest.

Again, it is said that if one of them dies
the other never mates again in this world; they
go through the world without a companion and
sit and sing the song of the lonely dove, until
it will melt your heart to listen to their song.
But some have said that, if the doves never mate
again, if there were any meaning to it, if a man
or woman either were to lose a companion, that
they could never marry again. But look at it
in its spiritual meaning, for it has a spiritual
application and not a worldly. I have known
men and women to lose their companions and
God could give them somebody else to love them
and comfort them and cheer them as they went
along through this world. The white dove is
a type of the Holy Ghost, and when the Holy
Ghost comes into your heart as your abiding
Comforter you are married, in the spiritual sense.
Now you and the Holy Ghost are life companions,
and now you talk more to the Holy Ghost than
you do to anybody else, and now your interest
is the same; you hunt such things as the other

loves, and you look after the things of the Holy
Ghost, and the Holy Ghost looks after the things
of yours, and if you grieve Him away you will
never be able to mate up with this old world
again and be happy, but you will be like the
lonely dove, you will sit and weep over the de-
parted one and you will sing your lonely song
and never be happy again until the White Dove
comes back into your heart and sits on the limbs
of the tree of life and sings you to sleep at night;
then you will be happy, and not until then.

So, beloved, never grieve the Holy Ghost
until He leaves you; keep the White Dove there
and make love to Him at all times. Let everything in the universe slip, but keep the Dove of
perfect love a-singing in your heart. Go to the
woods with Him, or to the flower-garden, or to
the poorhouse, or anywhere that He wants to
go. You may rest assured that, if you will never
break His companionship, you will never go into
sin, for that is one place that He will never go,
and if you go you will have to go alone, for
there He won't go. Never break with Him, beloved; let Him sing you to sleep every night.

CHAPTER VII.

CHRISTIAN PERFECTION.

Dear fellow-travelers, we want to talk to you to-day about Christian perfection. Our text is 1 Cor. 2: 6: "Howbeit we speak wisdom among them that are perfect."

When this text is quoted, there is a buzzing and a hissing among the unbelievers, and they grow eloquent in telling us what the Bible says. "Oh, yes," they say, "the Bible says 'there is none good, no not one,'" and they say that the Bible says, "He that saith that he liveth and sinneth not is a liar, and the truth is not in him." We might answer and say, "Oh, yes, the modern pulpits have taken all the fire out of Hell, and old Mrs. Eddy, before she went out into darkness and blackness, said that Hell was no more than a summer resort, and Mr. Russell appears on the scene and gives us a lecture, 'To Hell and Back,' and makes Hell a kind of a training-school to just go down and stay awhile and get cultured and refined, and finally be brought on

up to Heaven during your second probation."
But when the world is on fire, and the Judgment
Day has arrived, all of the above will go up in
smoke, but after all is done and said, the old
Book steps to the front and says, "We speak
wisdom among them that are perfect."

Now we hear from another crowd and they
tell us of at least a dozen different kinds of per-
fections that the text does not mean.   Well, we
are not discussing perfect shotguns, and we are
not discussing a perfect butcher-knife, but we are
discussing Christian perfection.   We believe
that when God convicts a sinner the conviction
is a perfect work, and we believe that when a
convicted sinner repents the repentance is perfect, and we believe that when a convicted sinner confesses his sins his confession is perfect,
and we believe that when a convicted sinner forsakes his sins the forsaking is perfect, and we
believe that when a convicted sinner believes
on the Lord Jesus Christ his faith is perfect, and
we believe that when God regenerates him the
work of regeneration is a perfect work; and we
believe now that the man receives the witness
of the Spirit that God gives him a conscious
knowledge of the fact that his sins are all forgiven, and that within itself is a perfect work;

and we believe that he is now adopted into the
family of God, and there is another perfect work;
and then we believe that he is now a son of God
and has everlasting life, and that now he can
consecrate himself upon God's altar a living sac-
rifice, soul and spirit and body, and that when
he does that God will give him the baptism with
the Holy Ghost and fire, and that will sanctify
him wholly and all sin, actual and inbred, is
taken out of him, and that makes him a perfect
Christian gentleman—not an angel or a God,
but a perfect Christian.   Now, beloved reader,
who do you decide with, the writer or the unbelievers?   What do you say about it?

The devil told you that Christian perfection
was a ghost and a scarecrow, a fog and a mist,
but he lied about it; it is the most beautiful thing
in all the wide world and the most real thing
to all those that are willing to pay the price
and take the goods.

Well, now for a little while I want to show
you that the Book teaches that everything that
goes to make up the Christian experience can be
made perfect.   First we will look at 1 John
4: 17: "Herein is our love made perfect, that we
may have boldness in the day of judgment: because as He is, so are we in this world."

Here the reader will see at a glance that the backbone of the Christlife and experience is love, and also that the Book says that our love can be made perfect, and the real meaning of the text is this. He means here that everything contrary to the love of God in the heart of His child can be removed, leaving the perfect love of God to reign in your heart without a rival. Well, glory to His name! To just think that that is possible is enough to make us shout for a thousand years.

Again, perfect love means that God gave His best for me, and that when I enjoy perfect love I will do my best for Him. Divine love gave all and Divine love requires all. God gave the best and we give our best. When the heart is filled with the perfect love of God, there is no anger or jealousy in the life, the life is perfectly transparent, nothing below the board, honest to the core, straight inside and out, clean inside and out; in fact, a walking gentleman.

We are told that this love will enable a person to love God with all the heart and all the soul and all the mind and all the strength, and your neighbor as yourself, and Christ said, "This do and thou shalt live." So we see how very necessary it is then that we have perfect love.

But we take another step. We next notice that our faith can be made perfect. See 1 Thess. 3: 10: "Night and day praying exceedingly that we might see your face, and might perfect that which is lacking in your faith."

Here the beloved apostle tells us that our faith can be made perfect, and we notice that at least two things are necessary to make up a perfect faith, we must have faith for pardon and we must have faith for a perfect cleansing, for it takes pardon and purity both to prepare us for Heaven. Heaven is a prepared place, and none but the prepared can get into that lovely city, for we read that nothing that defileth and worketh abomination or maketh a lie can enter there. Every step in divine life is taken by faith, and faith only, so our faith for pardon must be a perfect faith or the results won't come. And then, in addition to this, we must have a perfect faith for the cleansing of our natures and the purifying of our hearts. We must be a holy people, and He said a peculiar people zealous of good works, and that will be the natural result if we have perfect love and a perfect faith.

We next notice that our holiness is to be made

perfect. We read in 2 Cor. 7: 1: "Having therefore these promises, dearly beloved, let us cleanse
ourselves from all filthiness of the flesh and spirit,
perfecting holiness in the fear of God."

In the above text the apostle says that our
holiness can be made perfect. I suppose that
he means by perfect holiness perfect moral soundness, that we can be made perfectly sound morally, not one blemish in the moral side of a man's
life. A man may not be sound in his body, but
he can be sound in his morals. The Lord can
so clean up a fellow that there will not be a
speck of dirt in his whole life, and he will be
clean clear through and clear through he will
be clean. The eye of the Lord will run to and
fro in his life and find nothing to condemn, for
all the condemned stuff has been burnt out, and
the ashes sprinkled over the grave of the "old
man," and on the tombstone at the head of the
grave of the "old man" it will be "Holiness unto
the Lord," and at the gateway of the man's
soul it will be "Holiness unto the Lord."

The cleansing of the flesh and spirit goes before the perfecting of our holiness, clean inside
and out, that will not admit lodges or tobacco,
cards or the theater, or even the moving picture-
shows, that are looked on by many church-mem-

bers to be not only not sinful, but a great blessing. Some of the leading churches have gone so far as to put the moving pictures into their churches to take the place of the Sunday-night message, but not one poor soul will ever turn to the Lord from the moving-picture outfit, they can't trot Him out, He can't be found. There is nothing that will take the place of preaching the Gospel of Christ. The old Book says that "it pleased the Lord, by the foolishness of preaching, to save them that believe," and there is nothing that can take the place of preaching the Gospel by a holy man of God.

We next notice that we are to have perfect peace. In Isa. 26: 3, we read, "Thou wilt keep him in perfect peace, whose mind is stayed on Thee: because he trusteth in Thee."

Here we notice one of the crowning graces— perfect peace. It denotes the rest of the soul, an easy conscience and a contented mind. The reader will notice the absence of all fret and worry and struggling and stewing around about every little thing that comes up in life. Sin is an unrestful element, and as long as inbred sin reigns in the heart there is no such a thing as perfect peace. Inbred sin and perfect peace live in two different hearts, many miles apart, and have fellowship one with the other, but when that unrestful element, inbred sin, is removed, the peace of God that passeth all understanding will keep your heart and mind through Christ Jesus, and you will know what it is to rest in the Lord and enjoy perfect peace. The soul will be delivered from all that is unrestful, and when you speak of perfect peace, great quantities of joy will well up in the soul, and the soul will understand the meaning of the words "soul rest," or "full assurance," or "fulness of joy."

One meaning of the abiding Comforter is perfect peace, or perfect rest, or full deliverance; that is, delivered from all sin. In John 14: 27, we read the words of Jesus: "Peace I leave with you, my peace I give unto you: not as the world giveth, give I unto you. Let not your heart be troubled, neither let it be afraid." So we see again that the heart that is full of peace is delivered from trouble and fear, so says the Master; and Isaiah says it keeps the man, and Paul says it passeth all understanding, and in the 119th Psalm and 165th verse the Psalmist says that you can't offend the man with perfect peace. Just listen to King David: "Great peace have they which love Thy law: and nothing shall offend them." No flying off of the handle there, children.

We next notice that our patience is to be made perfect. We read in Jas. 1:4: "But let patience have her perfect work, that ye may be perfect and entire, wanting nothing."

I am of the opinion that the most of the people are just a little shorter on patience than on any other Christian grace. We seem, as a people, to be short there, and if we are lacking anywhere, it is on patience. We are not short at all on profession, we profess everything in the New Testament, and I have met some folks that professed some things that I never saw promised either in the Old or New Testament. But the apostle James says that we are to let our patience "have her perfect work, that we may be perfect and entire, wanting nothing." This text holds up the highest standard in the New Testament, and before it can be fulfilled we must have all that has gone before; we must have perfect love, and perfect faith, and perfect holiness, and perfect peace, and these Christian graces all combined will produce in you perfect patience, which is one of the most beautiful graces that can be found in the life of a Christian. Nothing is so unbecoming a Christian as a spell of impatience, and nothing so common with the average church-member as a regular spell.

Of course sometimes, as a people, we try to cover the thing up by calling it nervousness, and in some cases they do resemble each other. Impatience and nervousness are twin brothers, and look a good deal alike, but their headquarters are in two altogether different localities; one is located in a carnal heart, while the other is located in the nervous system. A man or woman under fire of the devil and tried to the very bottom, and yet patient and kind and gentle, has the most beautiful grace that a person can be in possession of. It is said of a soldier that the hardest trial of his life is to obey orders and stand still and watch the enemy approach, to hear the crack of the rifles of the on-coming army and have to stand perfectly still and keep patient under fire. If he could just be allowed to draw his sword and charge the enemy, it would be royal fun for him, but to have orders from headquarters to stand still and see the enemy approach, to hold steady and keep perfectly patient is no easy task.

One of the ways that our Leader tries us is to put us under the fire of the devil, and not allow us to shoot or even talk back or even defend ourselves. Sometimes when the devil has filled our good name with bullets, and hung our reputation up and thrown mud all over it, and the people say, "Oh, yes, if he wasn't guilty, he would clear that thing up and make an explanation," then the orders come back from headquarters, "Hold your peace, keep quiet, let the other crowd do the talking, don't defend yourself, you are Mine and it is My business to look after you." Then we listen and we hear James say, in the fifth verse of this same chapter, "If any of you lack wisdom, let him ask of God, that giveth to all men liberally, and upbraideth not; and it shall be given him." Wisdom to keep our mouths shut is a great gift, not many have it. Patience to keep sweet under the test is beautiful, I wonder if the reader has it.

Now we come to the next point. We are told that our works can be made perfect. We read in Heb. 13: 20, 21: "Now the God of peace, that brought again from the dead our Lord Jesus, that great shepherd of the sheep, through the blood of the everlasting covenant, make you perfect in every good work to do His will, working in you that which is wellpleasing in His sight, through Jesus Christ; to whom be glory for ever and ever. Amen."

Here the reader will see that the apostle says that our works are to be made perfect. When we think of perfect works, it looks like we are putting up the standard a little too high, but then we remember that it was not us that put up the standard, it was the Lord, and if the Lord ever asked a man to do a certain thing and did not furnish him with the grace to do it with, the man could fail and at the Judgment bar hold the Lord responsible for this command when He had made no provisions for His children to do the thing, and their obligations would naturally fall back on the Lord. But we know that God never requires an impossibility of any man, and if God says that our works are to be made perfect, He has promised somewhere in His Word a sufficiency of grace to enable us to do it. Bless His dear name!

We notice in the above text that the God of peace that brought again from the dead our Lord Jesus that great shepherd of the sheep, is the one that is to make us perfect in every good work, and not we ourselves. When we think that the God who could resurrect Jesus and bring Him back from the dead is the one that is to

make us perfect in every good work, we see that
it don't look so unreasonable as it did before. I
am of the opinion that the apostle was afraid
that we might doubt it and say that we could not
be made perfect in every good work, and to
stop us there and hold us to the Bible standard,
he says that the God that brought again from
the dead the Lord Jesus, He is the one that is
to do it. He knew that the greater includes the
less; that is, if you have ten dollars in your pocket,
you have got fifty cents in your pocket, but if
you have fifty cents, you may not have ten dollars. We know that the man that can build a
Chicago skyscraper can build a pigpen, but plenty
of men can build a pigpen that never could build
a Chicago skyscraper. We know that the standing miracle of the Old Testament was the crossing of the Red Sea, for when the Lord wanted
to do something good and great for His people,
He always reminded them that He brought them
out of Egypt and through the Red Sea. Many
times He wanted to do something for them out
of the ordinary and He was afraid that they
would doubt His ability to do it, then He would
remind them that He opened the Red Sea and
brought them through dryshod. At the same
time, the same crossing that meant life and de-

liverance to them meant death and destruction to their enemies. So it does with us, glory to God! And the standing miracle of the New Testament is the resurrection of Jesus Christ. No greater miracle was ever performed in any age of the world or under any dispensation of the world. The resurrection of Jesus is to-day the standing miracle of all the earth, and if the unbelievers and sinners and God-haters and Christ-despisers and blood-rejecters could do away with His resurrection, they would hold a jubilee all over the world and all through the pit of Hell at the same time. And now the God that justified you, and the God that regenerated you, and the God that sanctified you, and the God that brought again our Lord Jesus from the dead, is the one that is to make you perfect in every good work, to do His will. I say, "Glory to God in the highest, and on earth peace, and good will toward men!" He can do it. Hallelujah!

We next notice that we are to be made perfect saints and perfect men. We read in Eph. 4: 11-16: "And He gave some, apostles; and some, prophets; and some, evangelists; and some, pastors and teachers; for the perfecting of the saints, for the work of the ministry, for the edifying of the body of Christ: till we all come in the unity of the faith, and of the knowledge of the Son of God, unto a perfect man, unto the measure of the stature of the fulness of Christ: that we henceforth be no more children, tossed to and fro, and carried about with every wind of doctrine, by the sleight of men, and cunning craftiness, whereby they lie in wait to deceive; but speaking the truth in love, may grow up into Him in all things, which is the head, even Christ: from whom the whole body fitly joined together and compacted by that which every joint supplieth, according to the effectual working in the measure of every part, maketh increase of the body unto the edifying of itself in love."

We have given you a long quotation in order to make it real plain, for nobody can make a thing plainer than the Bible has already made it. The reader will see at a glance that the reason that the Lord gave us a diversified ministry was not to get sinners converted, but it was in order that the saints might be made perfect. Of course a saint is not a sinner, and if saints are to be made perfect, that proves that conversion or pardon, as powerful as it is, is not, within itself, a perfect work; it is a perfect conversion, but not a perfect cleansing. The text proves that there is something in the saint that remains after the new birth that must be cleansed away, and the apostle called it "the perfecting of the saint," or the making of the saint perfect, and when the saint is made perfect then the apostle says that he is a perfect man. Then he adds that they "are no more children, tossed to and fro," and then he says that they can not be carried about by "every wind of doctrine and the cunning craftiness of men, whereby they lie in wait to deceive." And so we see the object that God had in perfecting saints; it was to establish them, and that is the greatest need in our age—a Christian experience that will establish men, get them through to the bottom and down on the Rock of Ages. We need a backbone as big as a sawlog and ribs like the sleepers under the church where we go to worship, and nothing will give them to us but the baptism with the Holy Ghost and fire, and then we will have what the writter here called the "perfecting of the saints," or the making of perfect men, and that is nothing more nor less than a wholly sanctified believer.

CHAPTER VIII.

The Blood of Christ; or, Our Hope of Heaven.

The lesson is from the eleventh to the twenty-second verses of the ninth chapter of Hebrews. The text, 1 Pet. 1: 18-20: "Forasmuch as ye know that ye were not redeemed with corruptible things, as silver and gold, from your vain conversation received by tradition from your fathers; but with the precious blood of Christ, as of a lamb without blemish and without spot· who verily was foreordained before the foundation of the world, but was manifest in these last times for you."

The reader will notice that we are redeemed by the blood of Christ and not by silver and gold; that is, the works of man. If we could redeem ourselves with the perishable things of this world, there would have been no use of the blessed Son of God coming into this world and shedding His blood on Calvary, but we could not do it. We were as hopelessly lost as a soul could be,

St. Paul said that we were lost and without God and without hope in the world. Now I want to show you that our only hope of Heaven is found in the blood of the Son of God. There is no other way for us to go up only by the blood; it is the blood-route or perish. I don't care how well raised you have been or anything about your cultured taste and "refinement" (as it is called nowadays), you must go to Heaven covered by the blood, or stay out, one or the other. You can take your choice between the blood of Christ and an eternity of outer darkness. There is not one road for me and another for you, we must go in on the same line, which is a double track—pardoned by the blood and sanctified by the blood. Every step in the divine life must be taken through the blood of Christ or not taken at all, for there is no other way to mount up, and if you will go with us through this discourse, we will show you that the blood-route is the only one, that not one step is possible only through the blood.

Now we notice that we were redeemed by the blood of Christ. Well, now, we read in the ninth of Hebrews, twenty-second verse, that without the shedding of blood there is no remission of sins. So you see it is impossible to ever get rid

of sin without the blood of Christ. Your prayers can't remove sin, your groans can't remove
the thing, your tears can't wash it away, your
good works can never cover sin, and all of your
righteousness is as filthy rags in His sight.   And
so the question naturally arises, "What shall we
do, for the Bible says all have sinned and come
short of the glory of God?"   Well, my beloved,
there is but one thing that can be done; that is,
to go to God through the Lord Jesus Christ and
let Him remember the dying groans of His Son,
and let Him get a fresh look at the blood, and
then He can be reconciled to you; that is the
only way out of this thing that we call "sin."
To just think that we can get out of it at all
is enough to cause us to shout for the next million years, "Redeemed by His blood!"

Remission by His blood is the gateway to that
beautiful city that we call "Heaven," and redemption is the provision for all men from all
sin, for all time to come.   We sing,

"What can make me whole again?
Nothing but the blood of Jesus.
Oh, precious is the flow
That makes me white as snow;
No other fount I know,
Nothing but the blood of Jesus,"

and we never sung a truer song in this world
than that, for

> "The blood, the blood is all my plea,
> Hallelujah, it cleanseth me!"

And now we read, in Eph. 1:7: "In whom
we have redemption through His blood, the forgiveness of sins, according to the riches of His
grace." And we read also, in Col. 1:14: "In
whom we have redemption through His blood,
even the forgiveness of sins." Just the same
words that we find in Eph. 1:7. You see at a
glance that the apostle was so much interested
in the Atonement, and the redemption of man,
that he wrote the exact words to two different
churches. Why would he have done that if he
had not thought that it was essential to their
hope of Heaven? The thing that I want you
to look at is this, the apostle links together the
redemption of man and the forgiving of his sins.
Notice the two texts just quoted: "In whom we
have redemption through His blood, the forgiveness of sins." Redemption and pardon linked
together just like the links of a chain; there is
redemption, and there is remission, and there is
pardon, and all by the blood of Jesus.

Now, if you will listen, you can hear the

Rev. L. L. Pickett sing the best song that he
ever wrote.

> "Sing about the blood of Jesus,
> Tell us of its cleansing power;
> We will ever love the story,
> Tell us of its cleansing power."

The Spirit will lead a convicted and guilty
sinner to the cross, and when he gets to the cross
he will see the blood, and our Father said, "When
I see the blood I will pass over you," and Moses
said, "The blood shall make an atonement for
your soul," and the Lord said, "Sprinkle the blood
on the two side posts and the upper doorpost."
The death angel was a-getting ready to start
from the Celestial City with the sword of the
Lord in his hand, and in every home that was
not covered by the blood was one found dead,
after the angel had passed through the land.
So you see how important it was on that occasion to have the blood sprinkled on the doorpost. And we hear the Son of God say, in Matt.
13: 41, 42, "The Son of man shall send forth
His angels, and they shall gather out of His
kingdom all things that offend, and them which
do iniquity; and shall cast them into a furnace
of fire: there shall be wailing and gnashing of

teeth." One very sure way to offend the Son of God is to reject His blood, and laugh at the Atonement, and treat His death with scorn. The reader will notice that the blessed Son of God did not say that these offenders had made a blunder and a very fatal mistake, He said that they were to be cast into a furnace of fire, and then He adds that there will be wailing, and gnashing of teeth. It is an awful picture, at the best construction that you can put on it.

But we take another step in this journey as we climb the ladder toward Heaven. We next notice, in the Book of Revelation, the first chapter, fifth verse: "Unto Him that loved us, and washed us from our sins in His own blood, and hath made us kings and priests unto God."

The reader will notice in this quotation that old familiar term "washing." How natural it is to think of washing, everything that gets dirty we think of washing it, and now the Lord wants us to see that we are unclean and that we must be washed from our sins and made white in the blood of the Lamb, and then He says that we will not only be clean, but we will be made kings and also priests unto God. Now we know that a king is one that rules, and sits on a throne, and that a priest is the one that offers up spiritual sacrifices, and the Lord, in the above text, proposes to make us clean, and then make us kings and then priests.

In regard to the sin question, no word occurs oftener than the word wash; all through the Old and New Testaments the word is used in dealing with the slimy, dirty, greasy, filthy thing that the Book calls "sin;" it has gone into hundreds of the best hymns that were ever written, there is no hymn-book that does not contain a number of hymns on the subject of washing, and hence we are not surprised to hear the apostle say, "Now unto Him that loved us and washed us from our sins in His own blood, and made us kings and priests unto God and the Lamb." We know that a clean man is the greatest ruler on the face of the earth, and we know also that no man is a king, in the scriptural sense, except a clean man, and we know that no man can offer up spiritual sacrifices only a clean man; when he is washed and made clean he is then ready to do anything on earth or to go to Heaven, as the case may be.

But there are so many beautiful texts on the blood that we will now give you another to look at. We have now had redemption, remission, pardon and washing; we now look at justification. We see that there is but one way to stand before God justified, and that is by the blood of Christ. In proof of that statement, look at Rom. 5:9, and see for yourself: "Much more then, being now justified by His blood, we shall be saved from wrath through Him."

Here the reader will see at a glance that the only way of justification is by the blood. However, we read in this same chapter, in the first verse, that we are justified by faith. Well, Christ shed the blood and we exercise the faith. We could not shed the blood and He could not exercise the faith; our blood and His faith could never save a soul, but His blood and our faith can do wonders. Glory to His dear name for the possibilities of faith in the atoning blood of the Lamb! It is impossible for any one to go to Heaven without first being justified.

And so we see that Christ made provision for every step in divine life by His offering on the cross. When He said, "It is finished," He meant that a way had been opened up for man to escape the penalty of sin and to stand reconciled to God, but we must remember that nothing like that could ever have taken place without the shedding of the blood of the blessed Son of God, therefore how hard and cruel and wicked and devilish the man must be that can come before the world of dying men and make fun of the blood of the blessed Son of God and offer them a salvation on other grounds than those that God and Christ have provided.

Well now, we believe that a man that is justified is a member of the Church of Christ, and we hear a great deal of talk of the Church of Christ.

Well, Amen! He has one, and in fact the only one, and the orthodox churches of the land are all branches of the vine. We believe that thousands of precious souls have gone to Heaven from them all, but no church can claim to be the Church of Christ, and the only one, for one church is almost as good as another at the present time, or at least there is not much difference in them, but the man that is truly without a doubt holds membership in the real Church, and the real one belongs to the Son of God, and He has never turned it over to the Methodists or Baptists or the Presbyterians or anybody else. Thank the Lord He will work with us all and it is a fact that when we stop He goes on, and I say Amen!

"Well," somebody may say, "how did He get in possession of the Church?" Well, if you will

turn to the twentieth chapter of Acts, and read
the twenty-eight verse, you will have it in a nut-
shell. Now just turn and read it with me, and
we will see for ourselves: "Take heed therefore
unto yourselves, and to all the flock, over the
which the Holy Ghost hath made you overseers,
to feed the Church of God, which He hath pur-
chased with His own blood."

Now the reader will see at a glance that the
Church belongs to the blessed Christ, and is not
a man-made affair; it is not human machinery
and is not a human instrument. The real Bible meaning of the Church of Christ is the breaking of the power of the devil from off of men,
the destruction of sin in man's heart and life,
and the setting up of the spiritual kingdom of
the Lord Jesus Christ in man's soul. Now, beloved, that may not be the definition that a great
scholar would give you, but I like mine all right.
Glory to God! I am almost tickled to death
now because I belong to such an institution. He
said Himself that "the gates of Hell shall not
prevail against it," and, thank God, we believe
it. Glory to His name!

Well, now, what object did Christ have in
view when He bought the Church? Well the
old Book tells us. We read it in Eph. 5: 25-27.

Now we will read it, and every doubt in your
mind will be swept away, if you really want to
know, and I believe that you do: "Husbands,
love your wives, even as Christ also loved the
Church, and gave Himself for it; that He might
sanctify and cleanse it with the washing of water
by the Word, that He might present it to Himself a glorious Church, not having spot, or wrinkle, or any such thing; but that it should be holy
and without blemish."

The reader will see here that the object that
Christ had in view when He bought the Church
and paid for it in blood was that He might sanctify it, so, then, the Church is to be sanctified.
That part of the subject is now settled and dis-
posed of, and we can take up another step in
the ladder. Now He says "sanctify and cleanse
it," so the Church is to be a clean institution, and
then He adds, "and make it holy," so you see
it is to be sanctified and made clean and then
made holy. And then it is to be "without spot
or wrinkle," or blemish or any such thing, and
then He is to present it to Himself a glorious
Church. Just how much that all means is almost too much for man, and yet man can enjoy it all. Bless His holy name! I am so glad
that there is a power behind the Church that

makes it more than a conqueror, and the man
that is in it is in no danger as long as he stays
in the fold; there is no power on earth or in the
pit that can harm him, and I thank God the
devil knows it and so do you.   That is our hope
and stay, and our abiding place, and we sing,

> "My feet have found the resting place,
>   I am on the Rock at last."

We next notice that John says that we are
to be cleansed from all sin. If you will turn
to John's First Epistle, 1:7, we will read: "If
we walk in the light, as He is in the light, we
have fellowship one with another, and the blood
of Jesus Christ His Son cleanseth us from all
sin."

The reader will notice that when the blood
has been applied to the heart of the believer,
there is no sin left. The text says that the blood
cleanseth us from all sin, and the word *all* don't
mean *a part*, or *the most of it,* for it says all sin,
the whole lump, so the last and least remains of
sin are removed from the heart of the believing
Christian. We know that the text don't mean
the unregenerated sinner, for it speaks of the
fellow a-walking in the light as He is in the
light, and Christ and the justified believer are

neither one in the dark, but are both in the light. And the teaching of the Bible is that the sinner is in darkness until now, and in him is no light at all. If that is true, then the text is addressed to the justified believer, and, that being the case, then the justified believer is to be cleansed from all sin, and, that being the case, these two things are proven by the text, here they are—the justified believer has sin to be cleansed of, and, second, he can get the sin cleansed away.

That makes the cleansing a second work of grace, for the cleansing was applied to a man that was already justified, and that, within itself, proves that the great Holiness Movement is scriptural, right, and orthodox. As long as we preach that sinners must be converted and believers must be cleansed, we are doing our country a great service, for as long as the sinner is in sin he is in great danger of losing his precious soul, and as long as the believer has the carnal mind in his heart, he is in great danger of backsliding, and going back to the flesh-pots of Egypt. The Israelites said, while in the wilderness, "We do remember the cucumbers and the onions and the garlick," and they wanted to go back to Egypt.

We next notice that we are to enter into the
holiest of all by the blood of Jesus. Turn with
me to Heb. 10: 19, 20: "Having therefore, brethren, boldness to enter into the holiest by the
blood of Jesus, by a new and living way, which
He hath consecrated for us, through the vail,
that is to say, His flesh."

Here the reader will notice that the apostle
draws his lesson from the tabernacle in the wilderness. You remember that there was an outer
court, all classes could gather there; but
there was a gate, or a vail, that led into the Holy
Place, and the sinner could not get into that
place while he clung to sin, but only the believing
Jew was allowed there; but you will also remember that there was another gate, or vail, and
that led into the Most Holy Place, and nobody
could get into that place but the priest, and he
had to be sprinkled with blood for himself and
the people, and then he could only go into the
Most Holy Place once in a year.   .

But now the apostle tells us that we can go
into the holiest of all, and he also tells us how we
can do it. He says that Christ has made a way
by the shedding of His blood that will open up
the way into the holiest of all, and he calls
it a "new and living way," which is consecrated

for us. Now if I wanted to be made holy, and
there was no way by which it could be done,
that would be a great pity, and a slam on me,
but if the Lord has made a way by which He
can make me a holy man, and I refuse to let Him
do it, that looks like that would be a still greater
pity. Don't it make you feel sad to see the
Church all around a-talking about what they
would love to have, and then talking as though
there is no way to make them what they ought
to be? A poor man told me the other day that
God could not make him a holy man in this
world, that such a thing was impossible. Without a doubt the devil and the man's unbelief had
closed the door to him, and he is as much on the
outside as if the Lord was not able to do it for
him.

The next round in the ladder is Heb. 13: 12:
"Wherefore Jesus also, that He might sanctify
the people with His own blood, suffered without
the gate. Let us go forth therefore unto Him
without the camp, bearing His reproach."

There is a danger-signal in the above text,
and it is the great danger of you becoming a
blood-rejecter. Now if I had shed my blood to
make you a holy man, and if you were to reject
it, you would be no worse off, or if you were

to accept it, you would be no better off, but how different it is when you think of the blessed Son of God a-shedding His blood to sanctify men and make them holy! And now, after He has done the thing, for them to deliberately and calmly, but surely, reject the blood and become blood-rejecters, there is a reproach to the experience of sanctification, and just why I don't know, but I know that it is there. If it were as popular to be a sanctified man as it is to be a lodge man, there would be tens of thousands of men in the next few months to seek and obtain the glorious experience of sanctification; the news would spread all over the universe in the next few weeks, and our altars would be full, but there is nothing on earth as popular as the lodge, and nothing on earth as unpopular as to be a holy man, to walk with the Lord in white, to clean out your mouth, take off your badge, give the Lord one-tenth of your money and then give out of your nine-tenths, and to witness to the experience of sanctification as a second work of grace. You may just put it down on the flyleaf of your brain-pan that the devil don't like you a little bit, and what he will do to you will be a plenty. Now that is a hint at what is meant in Heb. 13: 12. The very fact that holi-

ness is unpopular is one of the dangers of your
soul, for you can't see God without the blessing,
and to get it it will make you unpopular, and
you don't want to be on the unpopular side, therefore you are in great danger of becoming a
blood-rejecter, and losing your precious, immortal soul. Don't do it; fly to the blood at once.

The next round in the ladder is Heb. 13: 20,
21: "Now the God of peace, that brought again
from the dead our Lord Jesus, that great Shepherd of the sheep, through the blood of the everlasting covenant, make you perfect in every good
work to do His will, working in you that which
is wellpleasing in His sight, through Jesus
Christ; to whom be glory forever and ever.
Amen."

Now the reader will notice in the above text
that Christian perfection is brought out and held
up to the man as a privilege; not as a duty and
a bondage and a burden, but in deed and in truth
a blessed privilege. The writer said that you
were to be made perfect in every good work, and
he said that the God of peace was to make you
perfect. He never said that you could do the
thing yourself, but that the God that you were
at peace with was the one that would do the
thing for you, and if He does the work, who

are you that you should rise up and say that it could not be done? Who shall we believe, the Lord or man? Paul tells us that God can not lie, and because He could swear by no greater, He sware by Himself. Well, now, what was the oath? It is this, listen to it: "The oath which He sware to our father Abraham, that He would grant unto us, that we, being delivered out of the hand of our enemies, might serve Him without fear, in holiness and righteousness before Him, all the days of our life." (Luke 1: 73-75.)

There is nothing lovelier than Christian perfection to be found on the whole earth. It is the one thing needful for all the human family, and if the Lord has gone so far as to put Himself on oath that we could have the blessing, it looks like that we would just simply run after it and never stop until we got in possession of it, but instead of that, we find that many would run the other way if they thought that they were in danger of taking it. To many people it seems like no greater calamity could come on them than to be saved from all sin, to be made holy and filled with the perfect love of God.

Well, we have come to the next round in this remarkable ladder, whose top reaches Heaven,

for the blood of Christ is the only ladder that
will reach to Heaven, and it is climb this ladder
or not go up at all.　We now turn to 1 Pet. 1: 2-
5: "Elect according to the foreknowledge of
God the Father, through sanctification of the
Spirit, unto obedience and sprinkling of the blood
of Jesus Christ; Grace unto you, and peace, be
multiplied.　Blessed be the God and Father of
our Lord Jesus Christ, which according to His
abundant mercy hath begotten us again unto a
lively hope by the resurrection of Jesus Christ
from the dead, to an inheritance incorruptible,
and undefiled, and that fadeth not away, reserved
in Heaven for you, who are kept by the power
of God through faith unto salvation, ready to
be revealed in the last time."

Now the reader will see at a glance that the
blood of Christ stands behind our election.　I
think all sanctified people are the elect people
of God, and are the one crowd that is ready
for the return of the Son of God, and therefore
they are called the "elect."　You will remember
that the apostle said, "Elect according to the
foreknowledge of God the Father, through sanctification of the Spirit, unto obedience and sprinkling of the blood of Jesus Christ."　The reader
will remember that Christ said that the Holy

Ghost could not be given until He was glorified, and of course He could not be glorified until He was crucified, and when He was crucified, then and there He shed His blood, and through the shedding of the blood of the Son of God the Holy Ghost could be given.   And when the Holy Ghost comes to the Church and the Church obeys, then the Father and the Son and the Holy Ghost all three vote for us, and the angels count the ballots, and it is unanimous, and the angels raise a shout on the other side and we raise a shout on this side, and then it is known in three worlds that we are the elect children of God, and then you hear them say, "Saved, and sanctified, and kept, and watching for the coming of my Lord."

Well, we are now ready to climb the next round in the ladder, and you will turn with me to Rev. 12: 11: "And they overcame him by the blood of the Lamb, and by the word of their testimony; and they loved not their lives unto the death."

The reader will here see at a glance that the power behind the testimony is the blood of the Lamb.   Without the blood there could be no testimony, and no power to overcome the devil, for the meaning of the above text is this, "They overcame the devil by the blood of the Lamb,

and by the word of their testimony." It is a
well-known fact that the devil has no substitute
for the blood, and when the child of God hides
behind the blood of Christ and pleads its effi-
ciency, the devil always moves, and he moves in
a hurry; he can stand all the school that you
can give him, and all the logic and science that
a man of brains can pile up, but when a poor,
weak Christian gets down on his knees and, with
his cheeks all wet with tears, looks up into the
face of his heavenly Father, and pleads the blood
of the blessed Son of God, the devil has to go,
and no imps will roost on his headboard for several days.   His hope is the blood, not the blood
and several other things that he might use to
a good advantage, but the blood is the remedy
for all the effects of sin in the human soul.
Schooling, and money, and social standing, and
good friends, and good standing, all may help
the man in this world, and they will, but at the
same time the man without any one of these
good things can get down on his knees in a cabin,
with poverty and crime and ignorance all about
him, and confess and forsake his sins, and plead
the blood of the Son of God, and hear from
Heaven just as quick as the other fellow.   No
man nor set of men has any control over the

blood of Christ or its power to save, and no sinner has to take it second-handed, he can go to headquarters for himself and plead his own case, and the reason is he understands his case better than the other fellow.

Well, now we come to the last round in the ladder. If you will turn to Rev. 7: 14, you will have the last text: "And I said unto him, Sir, thou knowest. And he said to me, These are they which came out of great tribulation, and have washed their robes, and have made them white in the blood of the Lamb."

Now the reader will notice that, to join the heavenly army, we must be washed in the blood of the Lamb, for it is the only hope of the sinner and the only hope of the Church. To join the blood-washed army will be no small affair. You see that the statement is not overdrawn when I say that our only hope of Heaven is in the blood of Christ. First, we saw that we were redeemed by the blood of Christ (1 Pet. 1: 18-20); second, that without the shedding of blood there is no remission of sin (Heb. 9: 22); third, we saw that we are pardoned by the blood of Christ (Eph. 1: 7); fourth, we saw that we were washed by the blood of Christ (Rev. 1: 5); fifth, we see that we are justified by the blood of Christ

(Rom. 5:9); sixth, we see that we have church membership through the blood of Christ (Acts 20:28); seventh, we see that we are cleansed by the blood of Christ (1 John 1:7); eighth, we see that we are made holy by the blood of Christ (Heb. 10:19); ninth, we see that we are sanctified by the blood of Christ (Heb. 13:12); tenth, we see that we are made perfect in love by the blood of Christ (Heb. 13:20, 21); eleventh, we see that we are elected by the blood of Christ (1 Pet. 1:2-5); twelfth, we see that we overcome the devil by the blood of the Lamb (Rev. 12:11); and thirteenth, we see that we join the blood-washed army only through the blood of the Lamb (Rev. 7:14). Now, reader, if you are not satisfied with the bill of fare, if you will let me know, I will send you another supply by return mail. The grace of the Lord Jesus Christ abide with you forever and ever. Amen!

CHAPTER IX.

The Holy Anointing Oil.

Dear reader, we want to talk to you about the holy anointing oil. We find it described so beautifully in the thirtieth chapter of Exodus, from the twenty-second verse to the close of the chapter. This will be a long text, but it is not too long, and there is not a verse that we can leave out of this beautiful lesson: "Moreover, the Lord spake unto Moses, saying, Take thou also unto thee principal spices, of pure myrrh five hundred shekels, and of sweet cinnamon half so much, even two hundred and fifty shekels, and of sweet calamus two hundred and fifty shekels, and of cassia five hundred shekels, after the shekel of the sanctuary, and of oil olive an hin: and thou shalt make it an oil of holy ointment, an ointment compound after the art of the apothecary: it shall be an holy anointing oil. And thou shalt anoint the tabernacle of the congregation therewith, and the ark of the testimony, and the table and all his vessels, and the candlestick

165

and his vessels, and the altar of incense, and the altar of burnt offering with all his vessels, and the laver and his foot. And thou shalt sanctify them, that they may be most holy: whatsoever toucheth them shall be holy. And thou shalt anoint Aaron and his sons, and consecrate them, that they may minister unto Me in the priest's office. And thou shalt speak unto the children of Israel, saying, This shall be an holy anointing oil unto Me throughout your generations. Upon man's flesh shall it not be poured; neither shall ye make any other like it, after the composition of it: it is holy, and it shall be holy unto you. Whosoever compoundeth any like it, or whosoever putteth any of it upon a stranger, shall even be cut off from his people. And the Lord said unto Moses, Take unto thee sweet spices, stacte, and onycha, and galbanum; these sweet spices with pure frankincense: of each shall there be a like weight: and thou shalt make it a perfume, a confection after the art of the apothecary, tempered together, pure and holy: and thou shalt beat some of it very small, and put of it before the testimony in the tabernacle of the congregation, where I will meet with thee: it shall be unto you most holy. And as for the perfume which thou shalt make, ye shall not make to your-

selves according to the composition thereof: it
shall be unto thee holy for the Lord. Whosoever
shall make like unto that, to smell thereto, shall
even be cut off from his people."

The reader will see at a glance that the holy
anointing oil is a type of the Holy Ghost. This
holy anointing oil was not to be put on everybody; there were but three classes of people that
this oil could be put upon, and they were the
priests, and the prophets, and the kings.   It
could not be put on the entire crowd of people,
and it was not to be put on a stranger. The
stranger there is a type of the sinner in our day,
and the sinner cannot receive the Holy Ghost in
this age of the world. He must first receive the
pardon of his sins, and then he is made a priest
and a prophet and a king, and now after that
takes place he is in condition to receive the Holy
Ghost, which this holy anointing oil stands for
in the beautiful lesson that we have just read.

We read in the Book of Revelation, 1: 5, 6:
"Unto Him that loved us, and washed us from
our sins in His own blood, and hath made us
kings and priests unto God."   Hence we read
that the man that has been washed from his sins
was, in so doing, made a king and also a priest,

and we read again in the Book of Revelation that,
"The testimony of Jesus is the spirit of prophecy." (See Rev. 19: 10.) And all this proves
another thing, that God has never taken a sinner to consecrate him to the office of either priest
or prophet or king; He must have taken a saved
man, for the oil could not be applied to a stranger, which is the sinner. The new birth makes
us fit subjects for the baptism with the Holy
Ghost, and He never comes on the sinner, according to the words of Jesus in John 14: 15-17.
The reader will see in these verses that Jesus
makes a distinction between the Christian and
the sinner, one can receive Him and the other
can not. "If ye love Me, keep My commandments." Now that could not be said to a sinner, for a sinner don't love Jesus, and of course
don't keep His commandments.

But look at the next verse: "And I will pray
the Father, and He shall give you another Comforter, that He may abide with you forever."
Now notice the next verse: "Even the Spirit of
truth; whom the world cannot receive, because
it seeth Him not, neither knoweth Him:
but ye know Him; for He dwelleth with you,
and shall be in you." Here Jesus tells us that
the world cannot receive the Holy Ghost, and

He said that the disciples could receive Him, therefore they must have been saved people and fit subjects for the incoming of the Holy Ghost, or they would have been cut off as the rest of the world was. Of course the sinner is not cut off from Bible conviction, and Bible repentance, and Bible confession, and Bible forsaking, and Bible restitution, and Bible believing, and Bible receiving, for all his past guilt, but to say that the sinner can come to the Lord, make a consecration and receive the baptism with the Holy Ghost is not scriptural. But when he has been translated out of the kingdom of darkness into the kingdom of light, he is another man altogether, and now he is able to make his consecration and receive this holy anointing oil, and he is not only a consecrated man, but he is also an anointed man, for he has done his part, and the Lord has done His. Now we have before us the real thing, no make-believe about it, no sham, no half job, but the work is complete, for he has been born of the Spirit and also baptized with the Spirit. It takes the birth and the baptism both to complete the salvation of a man's soul; if the birth of the Spirit had have been all that the human family needed, the baptism with the Spirit never would have been provided for man. The Lord said to Moses, "This holy anointing oil shall not be put upon a stranger," and He also said that if a man put it upon a stranger that he was to be cut off.

The holy anointing oil is a type of the Holy Ghost in His lubricating powers. The oil will lubricate, and keep out friction, and keep down the hot-boxes, and keep off the rust, and keep the machinery in splendid running order; it keeps everything soft and pliable. It also puts on a shine. Nothing will make the face shine like the holy anointing oil. A man may be untrained, and naturally rough, and really ugly, but when he is filled to the overflowing with the Holy Ghost, he is good looking.

There are many beautiful symbols of the Holy Ghost in the old Book, the oil is only one of the many. He is described as water. We read in Ezek. 36: 25: "Then will I sprinkle clean water upon you, and ye shall be clean: from all your filthiness, and from all your idols, will I cleanse you."

Here the reader will see that the clean water is a type of the Holy Ghost. When it was applied to a person, he was cleansed from all his filthiness and from all his idols. This is a work of the Holy Ghost. That water there is not in a

sense the kind that we get out of the creek; the
common, literal water applied to a man could
not do what we read here was done, so we must
believe that the clean water here is a type of
the Holy Ghost, and that proves that the office
work of the Holy Ghost is to cleanse and make
pure. He said, "From all of your filthiness and
from all of your idols will I cleanse you." Notice, He said, "Then will I sprinkle clean water
upon you, and ye shall be clean." Not just a
little bit cleaner than you were before, but clean,
so that it is the work of the blessed Holy Ghost
to make clean and pure and holy, and to give
moral soundness clean clear through, and clear
through clean—no flies in the ointment at all.

Again we have a picture of the Holy Ghost
under the symbol of fire. You see we first had
oil, and second we had the water. and third we
have the fire. The oil is a picture of the Holy
Ghost as a lubricator, the water as a purifier
and a life giver, and the fire shows Him as a
purifier and a refiner. There is nothing that
consumes like fire. It takes the fire to get rid of the
proud flesh and the self. It is remarkable how
big some people are until they get the fire from
Heaven, and then it is remarkable how small
they are. You saw them a few days ago and

there was a puff and strut and spouting until you could hardly stand them, their nose was in the air and their chin was almost in the clouds, but they meet with God in His wonderful power, and the blessed Holy Ghost is applied to their hearts, and they are made clean and holy and all the dross and tin are removed, and now when you look at them, you see nothing but a little pile of ashes; the puff and strut is all taken out, and, behold! they are just natural human beings, and they look like other folks, and they feel that they are not as good as other folks, and now they are surprised to think that God has put up with them at all, and they are just simply amazed.

The fire is wonderful in its power to destroy things, and Paul said that the "old man" was to be crucified, and that the body of sin was to be destroyed. A crucifixion looks like a cross, but a destruction looks like a fire. When you go to town and they tell you that they have had a big fire, you can't always tell how big the fire was by what you see, but more often you tell how big the fire was by what you can't see. If you see a great deal, you know that the fire was not very large, but if you don't see much, you know that the fire was truly a big one.

Fire is awful hard on rats and rag roses; it just burns them clear off, and then burns them up. It is also hard on earrings; I have seen them melted off that had cost hundreds of dollars. When the fire breaks out, earrings and finger-rings and chains and bracelets and pipes and cigar-cases, and such like, always burn up. And again, the fire from Heaven is awful hard on the chain link and the square and the letter G and the elk head and the chopping-ax. They just can't stand the fire at all; they are consumed at once and become as dross and tin. The change is something wonderful—an elk's head one day, and a man's head the next.

Again, we find that the wind is another symbol of the Holy Ghost. There are oil and water and fire and wind; the oil is a lubricator, the fire is a consumer, the water is a life-giver and a purifier, and the wind shows the life-giving energies of the Holy Ghost.

There is no living at all without the wind. We can live for some time without water, but we must have wind right now or die, and the wind is one of the life-giving energies of the Holy Ghost. "When the day of Pentecost was fully come, they were all with one accord in one place. And suddenly there came a sound

from Heaven, as of a rushing mighty wind, and
it filled all the house where they were sitting.
And there appeared unto them cloven tongues,
like as of fire, and it sat upon each of them: and
they were all filled with the Holy Ghost, and began to speak with other tongues, as the Spirit
gave them utterance." There we have both fire
and wind in the above text. Life and purity are
both seen in the above text. The Holy Ghost
as wind gave them life from above, and the fire
gave them purity and power. The man with the
life can get up and move, and the man with the
fire can burn his way through the hard places,
melt out the icebergs and melt down the cold,
frozen pulpits. The hardest thing to preach
over is a frozen pulpit; you can preach over
almost anything else, but when you find a froz-
en-up pulpit, it is something awful to try to thaw
out and burn up and melt out, and we might
keep on a-saying, but it is a fact that when the
church is without fire the pulpit is always frozen
up. No church is without fire if there is plenty
in the pulpit, and if the pulpit is without it,
it is not the Lord's fault, for He has all the
fire that we can use.

Again we see that the Holy Ghost is said to
be our abiding Comforter. He is to comfort,

and console, and soothe, and abide with us. He
said that He would not leave us comfortless, or
He would not leave us orphans (which is said
to be the real meaning of the word). Well,
Amen! Then we are not left to grope out a miserable existence here in this world, but the Holy
Ghost is to abide with us as our abiding guest,
and no soul can be lonesome or sad with such
company as the blessed Holy Ghost.

And He is to be more than just our Comforter, He is to be out Teacher. Christ said
that when the Holy Ghost comes He will teach
us all things, and, more than that, He is not
just to teach us; the Lord said that He would
bring all things to our remembrance, "Whatsoever I have said unto you." So, then, we th'nk
of Him as oil, and as water, and as fire, and as
wind, and as our Comforter, and our Teacher,
and also as our Revealer.

He is to take the things of Christ and reveal
them unto us, and one of the things that He is
to show us is that the Son of God is divine. No
man that has ever received the Holy Ghost can
doubt that Christ is divine, and the crowd in
this country that is doubting the divinity of
Christ has never received the Holy Ghost; they
are strangers to Christ, for when the Holy Ghost

comes to abide in us, He is to take the things
of Christ and show them unto us, for that is
to be the work of the Holy Ghost. And when
He is come, the doubts are a thing of the past,
and the darkness is no more a-hanging over your
head, but the light of Heaven is a-shining in
your soul, the glory of God is your watchword,
Amen! is your password, and the enemy is no
longer able to keep you in doubt about the divinity of Christ or the inspiration of the Holy Scriptures; you know that Christ is the divine Son of
God and that the Bible is the inspired Word of
God. Nothing but the Holy Ghost can make all
of these things real to us, but, bless the Lord!
He can do it.

The mystery of one God is no mystery to
a saved and sanctified man. In his mind, and
also in his heart, he can see God the Father and
God the Son and God the Holy Ghost, and the
blessed Holy Spirit has revealed the Father and
Son both to him so clearly that it is as easy
to believe as it is to breathe; it is perfectly natural to believe God, and to believe the Bible,
and to take what we have sometimes called the
"lonely way" with the Holy Ghost, but that
don't mean that we are in a way that is lonely,
for the way is not lonesome or lonely, for we

have the abiding Comforter. And He is continually taking the things of Christ and showing them to us, and we are so interested in what
our teacher is a-teaching us that we are everything above ground but lonesome; we could not
get lonesome, our soul has found its resting-
place and we are a-resting in Jesus. And then
it is natural for us to sing:

> "Singing I go along life's road,
> Praising the Lord, praising the Lord.
> Singing I go along life's road,
> For Jesus has lifted my load."

Well I say, glory to God for the thought that
the blessed Holy Spirit comes as the anointing oil,
and then He comes as the water of life, and
then He comes as the purifying fire, and then
He comes as a rushing, mighty wind, and He
fills us with the life-giving energy, and puts an
eternal "go through" in us, until nothing looks
hard to us, and we go up and down in this country singing as we go that the Comforter has
come, and, more than that, our blessed Teacher
has come, and, more than that, that our blessed
Revealer has come. He now takes us in hand,
and fires the soul, and touches the mind, and
quickens the body, and prepares us for the duties

and the responsibilities of life, and no man is prepared for these things until he is filled with the Holy Spirit, and made clean and holy and Christlike.

CHAPTER X.

Dear reader, we want to talk to you about the dangers of your soul, and for a text we use several Scriptures. First, Ezek. 18: 4, and also 18: 20, and Matt. 16: 26, and Luke 12: 20, and Mark 8: 36, 37. Mark says: "For what shall it profit a man, if he shall gain the whole world, and lose his own soul? Or what shall a man give in exchange for his soul?"

This text, with the other four, teaches that a man may lose his soul. The very thought is enough to scare a man to death, and take his breath, and if a man's soul may be lost there is danger of it, and if there is a danger (and there is, for the Book say so), then we ought to go to work to see if we can find out the dangers and just what they are. We will take them up one at a time, as they come to us, and show you what we think are a few of the leading dangers of the human soul.

The first one that we will notice is seen in

179

the fact that the child is born into the world with
the carnal mind in it, and the carnal mind is one
of the greatest dangers of the human soul, and,
in fact, it is the chief danger.   There are other
dangers, of course, but the carnal mind is the
chief one.   The child comes into this world with
the carnal mind in it, and when it is young, the
child kicks and screams, and as he gets older
he screams and kicks and fights and bites, and
as he gets older he drinks and cusses and murders and lies and steals and often finds a place
in the state prison or on the gallows or in the
fatal chair, and if the blood of a crucified Savior
is not applied to the heart, it will finally put him
in outer darkness, and it will rob him of his soul,
and finally rob him of Heaven.

For a scriptural proof of depravity, see Isa.
1: 5, 6: "Why should ye be stricken any more?
ye will revolt more and more.   The whole head
is sick, and the whole heart faint.   From the
sole of the foot even unto the head there is no
soundness in it; but wounds, and bruises, and
putrifying sores: they have not been closed,
neither bound up, neither mollified with ointment."

Now, reader, that is the real, inward condition of man as God sees him all along the jour-

ney of his life, but we only see it after the sore breaks out on him as we look at him in the gutter or the jail or the prison or in the fatal chair. We throw up our hands and say, "Who would have thought it!" Well, God said that the disease was there all the time, and He provided a remedy for all sin, and the man ignored the remedy and was led of the carnal mind and the death in the chair is just the natural result of the inbred depravity of his own heart. We look at the great multitude down town in the low places, and we say, "How vile!" We look at the crowd up town, and say, "How nice they are!" But God says that the heart of the sinner up town, is as bad as the heart of the sinner down town; by next year the down-town crowd will be in their graves, and the up-town crowd will be down to take their place. All of that is the working of the carnal mind, and proves that the heart of man is in a state of depravity, and nothing but the new birth can change his heart.

Again we read, in Ps. 51: 5: "Behold, I was shapen in iniquity, and in sin did my mother conceive me." Now, reader, there is a man with the same disease that all the rest of us have suffered with, and he was honest enough to acknowledge it. He said that he was born in that con-

dition, he did not say that he learned to do bad,
for that is one thing that no child has to learn,
it is born in it, and it does bad because it can't
do anything else. No child ever has to be taught
to lie, it tells lies by the score without ever being
taught. In Ezek. 18: 2, we read, "The fathers
have eaten sour grapes, and the children's teeth
are set on edge." That is another way to tell
us that the depravity of the child is handed down
to it from the parents, and it runs back to the
fall of man in the garden. And again we read,
in Ps. 58: 3: "The wicked are estranged from
the womb; they go astray as soon as they be
born, speaking lies."

Now, reader, you will see that the man that
wrote the above text says that the children had
manifestations of depravity as soon as they were
born. That is my experience. As far back as
my recollection goes, I had the marks of the
beast on me; before I was taught to do wrong,
the disease was already broken out, and it was
as natural to do wrong as it was to breathe.

But some may say that all the Scriptures that
we have quoted were in the Old Testament.
Well, that is true, but we have not kept out of
the New Testament because we find no Scriptures there that would teach that the heart is

depraved. We could almost make a book of quotations from the New Testament, but we will only look at a few. First look at Mark 7: 21-23: "For from within, out of the heart of men, proceed evil thoughts, adultery, fornications, murders, thefts, covetousness, wickedness, deceit, lasciviousness, an evil eye, blasphemy, pride, foolishness: all these evil things come from within, and defile the man." And the same awful picture is found in Gal. 5: 19-21, only it is a little worse in Galatians, if it were possible to make it worse. No sane man can read the above, and know that it was the words of the Son of God, and fail to see that the human family was in an awful condition, too far gone to ever recover itself. There is but one remedy, and only one, and that is in the blood of the Son of God.

But we will give the reader one other quotation from the New Testament, and leave it with you as we find it. Now turn to Eph. 2: 3, and read for yourself: "Among whom also we all had our conversation in times past in the lusts of our flesh, fulfilling the desires of the flesh and of the mind; and were by nature the children of wrath, even as others." Oh, brother, there is no use in putting on this corpse a tailor-made suit of clothes and passing him off for a live

man, for this fellow is a dead man, no make-
believe about it; he shows total depravity.

The next danger of your soul that we will
notice is this; the child, as soon as it is born into
this world and starts on the journey of life,
begins to form acquaintances, and they are not
always spiritual, and they have an awful power
over the child. The power of our associations
over us is one of the dangers of the soul, and
there are more boys and girls in the state prisons
and places of shame by the power of their associations than by any one power that has ever
been brought to the knowledge of man. While
it is true that all have the carnal mind in them,
at the same time about all the folks that I ever
met were more or less led by somebody else.
The power of friendship or association is a remarkable power over us, and we can't help it.
If our association was all good, it would be much
easier to live right than it is, for the child hardly
starts in life until the devil has some one on the
spot to help it to start in the wrong direction,
and also to make the wrong choice, and step
by step and choice by choice, it is led off by the
enemy until the life is a complete wreck, and the
steps that point in the wrong direction are only
another way of saying that the "old man" is on

the throne and the bridle in his hand. A boy
or girl that once gets out into the world, and
gets into the swim of society, and gets started
in the whirlpool of sin, it is next to impossible
to ever stop; their association is against them,
and nothing but the power of God can break the
awful grip of this world from off the necks of
the victims that are under the yoke of the devil.
Their own sinful nature is against them, and
the devil with all his power is against them, and
their association is against them, and this old
world as we see it is against them, and, sad to
say, in many places the preachers of the Gospel
of Christ will tell them that they can never be
delivered from the carnal mind in this life.

The next danger that we will notice is the
habits of men that they have acquired and
formed. These are their worst enemies. The
most of the human family are under bondage to
their own awful habits; they are the victims of
the devil, and also the victims of depravity, and
also the victims of their own selves. The average young man of America has so completely
sold himself out to the lower nature of man that
he is everything in the world but a free, happy
man. They are bound by the drink habit, and
the tobacco habit, and the habit of bad reading,

and Sunday baseball has been one of the means
of the devil in the United States to rob the people of their Christian Sabbath. The habit of
going to baseball on Sundays in the afternoons
has so fastened itself on men that they would
feel like they were robbed of all that is worth
living for if they could not drink and smoke and
go to Sunday baseball. And the ballrooms are
open every night almost, and the dancing-school
teachers are in as great demand as the preachers
of the Gospel in many of our cities, and then,
to cap the climax and to show off depravity to
a good advantage, the people of America have
put the Bible out of the public school and have
put in a dancing course, and your children are
to be taught how to dance. It matters nothing
as to what their parents think, they must take
their training and do their part of the dancing.

We will sum up a part of what we see and
know, and just say that as to the above situation
concerning the public school system of the United
States, that they have rejected God and the Bible
and God has rejected the public schools of America, and the darkest outlook for our country is
not now the prisons full of old, hardened criminals, but the nation around about us with seven-
teen million children in the public schools where

they are without a Bible. The old criminals will
all soon be dead and out of the way, but what
of the oncoming crop of children without God?

The next danger of your soul that we will
notice is the fact that "without holiness no man
shall see the Lord," and to be scripturally holy
and to profess the experience of sanctification is
one of the most unpopular things in the United
States. Nobody hardly wants to be on the unpopular side; they want to go with the crowd,
and they want to go where the crowd goes, and
see what the crowd sees, and do what the crowd
does, and the crowd has never been on the right
side of any question, the majority has always been
wrong and the minority has always been right
on the moral questions of the day. As it is very
unpopular to be holy, that is one of the greatest
dangers to the salvation of your soul that I ever
studied. How easy it is to drift with the tide,
and how hard it is to cut your way across the
wills and opinions of the folks and go up stream,
when all the associations of your earlier life are
a-drifting with the crowd, and they think strange
of you if you don't go with them, and they look
on you as one that is very weak and narrow and
too stupid to be of any worth to the world in
which you live. They are not holy, and don't

want to be, and don't expect to be, and they don't
want you to be, and if you are, it will make you
one of the most unpopular men in the eyes of
the world that can be found on the face of the
whole earth. Because it is so unpopular, that
is one of the great dangers of your soul, for
so few are willing to take the lonely way with
Jesus and let the world sneer at them as they
go by, and let the world snub them and hold them
up to ridicule, and pass them by on purpose,
just because they believe in the doctrine and experience of sanctification.   Well, beloved, not
very many will take the straight track and the
narrow way, and break with the world, and because of the reproach of the cross of Christ not
many will pay the price and go through, and so,
after all, one of the great dangers that we have
to face is the unpopularity of the thing. If it
was as popular to be holy as to be a lodge man,
all would be after it.

The next danger of your soul that we will
look at is the uncertainty of life. The very fact
that you must die and don't know when is one
of the dangers of your soul. The uncertainty of
life is enough to scare every sinner to death,
but it seems to have no effect on them at all,
they go right on in sin and open rebellion against

God, take the reins into their own hands and
travel in the direction of Hell at the rate of sixty
minutes to the hour.   They don't even get ex-
cited over it, and have no idea but what that
is their last hour, and in fact it may be, for as
the time is hid from us, we don't know but what
this breath is the last one.   We know that death
is on our track, and that the Judgment Day is
set, and eternity is in view, and no man has a
lease of his life; he is just a-passing through
this country and don't know when he will be
called out, but he does know that he will be
called, and as he don't know when, that is one
of the fearful dangers of his soul.

And the next danger that we look at is the
certainty of death.   While the uncertainty of life
is one of the great dangers of the soul, the certainty of death is another.   As truly as we are
here to-day, we are leaving here to-morrow.   We
don't know when we will go, but we do know
that we are going, and that before long, with a
preparation or without one, we will have to go
the very hour that we are called.   With these
facts before us, we ought to see to it before the
sun goes down that our peace is made with our
Maker.   How can we go out into darkness, without a light to guide us, or a hope of Heaven,

or without one word to the loved ones that would give them one ray of hope as to our salvation? How short is life and how long is eternity! A few days here and out there forever.

The uncertainty of life and the certainty of death are some of the dangers of our souls; of course not all of the dangers. They are many and fearful and dreadful, but the world is bound by the devil, and is so completely dominated by the devil, that they are dead to all of their dangers.

The last danger of your soul that we will speak of is the fearful fact that when the soul is lost it is lost forever; not so with anything else. You may lose your home and buy another, lose your horse and buy another, lose a friend and make a dozen to take the place of the one; but when the soul is lost, it is lost forever and ever. I know that we have some very brilliant men now in some of the churches that are offering the people a second probation; that is, that they can die in an unsaved state, go to the place of unrest and stay a few years or a few months, get trained and refined and cultured, and then have a second chance, accept it, and come on up to their eternal rest. I don't know on just what grounds they think they would accept it if they had a chance, for if a man rejects the first offer of mercy, goes on in sin and becomes harder and harder, and then goes down to the pit of darkness and stays a few years with the devil and the lost, I am of the opinion that he would not accept the second chance if he had one. And the Bible nowhere says that he is to have any. Christ says that "these shall go away into everlasting punishment, and the righteous into life eternal. One crowd goes away and the other goes in. Those that went out, went out forever, and those that went in, went in forever.

As we look at the awful dangers of our souls, we are made to stand and quake and tremble. The thought that the soul may be lost is an awful thought, but the depravity of the heart leads in that direction, our associates lead us in that direction, our habits lead us in the same way, and to be holy is unpopular, and you may not want to be with the unpopular crowd, and that is another fearful danger, and the uncertainty of life is another danger, and the certainty of death is another. And the fact that when the soul is lost it is lost forever is a danger that we don't understand and can't explain, but the dangers of the soul are many and fearful; just one hope—the Blood.

CHAPTER XI.

The Threefoldness of Salvation.

Dear reader, I want to talk to you about the threefoldness of salvation. That salvation is threefold in its length and breadth and depth and height no man that reads the Bible will deny. In the atonement Jesus provides a salvation that is threefold, and to make that plain to you just let me illustrate what I mean by threefoldness of salvation. First, when a man is regenerated, he is saved from the guilt of sin; and when he is sanctified, he is saved from inbred sin; and when he is glorified, he is saved from the presence of sin, and also the effects of sin. But you may say, "Where is the Book on that?" Well, I am just now ready to show the passages to you, that is, the three Scriptures that teach the threefoldness of salvation, and the threefoldness of salvation proves that sin is threefold in its aspect, or in its awful effect on the human family. Now the first salvation that we will look at is in Luke 1:77: "To give knowledge of salvation unto His people by the remisson of their sins." Now reader, in the above quotation you will see the first installment in salvation; it is a "salvation by the remission of their sins."

And now we will show you the second installment. Turn to 2 Thess. 2: 13: "But we are bound to give thanks alway to God for you, brethren beloved of the Lord, because God hath from the beginning chosen you to salvation through sanctification of the Spirit and belief of the truth." Here the reader will see very plainly the second installment in salvation; the first salvation was by the remission of their sins, and the second through sanctification of the Spirit and belief of the truth. The first came to sinners, for their sins had to be pardoned, and the second came to the "brethren beloved of the Lord," and they were Christians, and they had to be sanctified. So you see the sinner needs pardon and the believer needs sanctification.

Now we will show you the third installment in salvation. Will you turn to 2 Tim. 2: 10, and read with me, "Therefore I endure all things for the elect's sake, that they may obtain the salvation which is in Christ Jesus with eternal glory." The reader will see the third installment, which is a salvation with eternal glory, and this installment came to the elect.

Now we will go back and take a few minutes to look at each one of these salvations. The first was a salvation by the remission of their sins, and of course it came to sinners, and a sinner is a person that the Bible says is "dead in tresspasses and in sins," and if a man is dead, he is without life, and if he is without life, he is without activity. The sinner is as free from spiritual life as a corpse is from physical life. The sinner is dead to God, and dead to Christ, and dead to the Holy Ghost, and dead to the Church of Christ, and dead to his own eternal interest. And God said that the plowing of the wicked is sin, because he raises more wheat to buy more land with to raise more wheat on to buy more land with, in order that he may glorify himself instead of God. "God is not in all his thoughts," so says the old Book; it has never entered into his mind that the first duty of life is to glorify God, and the second is to help humanity, but he is his own sun and stars and moon, and rises and sets and changes and quarters and fulls all under his own hat and in his own breast; he is his own god, he bows to nobody but to his own self and selfishness, therefore if he ever gets to Heaven he must be changed. No tuining of a new leaf here, man, it must be a change; you must be a new creation, taken out of one world and taken up into another one. Paul says that God will deliver us from the power of darkness and translate us into the kingdom of His dear Son, and that is the thing that every unregenerated man on earth has to have to become a Christian. Nothing but the new birth will make a real Christian out of you. I have heard it said that to be converted was just to turn around, and again I have heard others say that to be converted was to just change your mind, but that won't work, for the devil turns around a thousand times a day, and he also changes his mind. Every time he tries to capture a fellow and fails, he at once changes his mind and also his plans, and goes to work in some other way to try to accomplish his devilish end. And yet he is not religious at all, that is, he has no salvation, for salvation means deliverance from sin, and the devil is a sinner, therefore he is without salvation.

But when a man is scripturally converted, he is regenerated, and that makes him a New Testament Christian, and now he is ready for the experience of sanctification, which is another salvation, or another work of grace. And the bless-

ing of sanctification don't deal with a man's actual
sins, it deals with the inbred sin that caused him
to commit sin, that had to be pardoned. The
work of regeneration is to impart new life to the
dead soul, to remove the guilt of sin and bring
the soul into touch with God until the eyes and
ears of the soul have been opened and the understanding has been quickened. And now the soul
can see and hear and understand and know God,
and have fellowship with Him.

That is indeed a very great work of grace,
so great that many have supposed that that was
all that God could do for the soul of man, but
that is only the beginning and not the end of
salvation. And now, in the second work of grace,
the heart is cleansed and made pure, the "old
man" is crucified, the body of sin destroyed, and
the soul is filled with the Holy Ghost and becomes
one of the elect children of God, for you will notice that when the sinner received the remission
of his sins he became the "brother beloved of the
Lord," and when the brother beloved of the Lord
was sanctified he became the elect.

And now we come to the biggest blessing that
can come to a human soul, and that is for the
elect to be glorified, for in this blessing the effect
of sin is forever removed from the soul and mind

and body, and not only the effect of sin is removed, but the glorified soul will never see any more sin while eternity rolls on, and that will be a greater work than even pardon or purity. And then just what Heaven will be no man can tell. We all have a few ideas of what Heaven is, and what it is like, but after we are glorified, we may never use those ideas again, we may dismiss them from our minds.

And the Bible not only speaks of the threefoldness of salvation, but it also speaks of only three places of abode—this world and Heaven and Hell. And there are three classes of people spoken of in the Bible—the sinner and the justified and the sanctified. There is no grace in the sinner at all, he is full of sin, and there is no grace in Hell, it is full of sin, therefore the sinner is the only type of Hell that we have on earth, and sometimes he gets so full of sin and Hell that he ends his life and goes to the pit to get more of the same thing that he was so full of here in this world. We all know that there is no good in Hell, and God said of the sinner that "there is none that doeth good, no not one."

And we find also that the regenerated man is a type of this world. This world is in a mixed state, it is not all bad, glad to say, but it is not all good, sorry to have to say, and the only type of this world that can be found on earth is a regenerated man, they are both in a mixed state. Sometimes you look at a regenerated man and you see the spiritual man on the throne, and, from what you can see, he will get to Heaven; in spite of the world and the flesh and the devil he is going to make it. But alas! in a few days you meet the same man and behold, the "old man" is on the throne, and from what you can see, the devil will get him in spite of the Father, Son and Holy Ghost.

The regenerated man is the man spoken of by the apostle Paul when he said, "But ye are yet carnal"—some good, some bad. But the wholly sanctified man is a type of Heaven, Heaven is all good and no bad. There is no sin in Heaven, either actual or inbred, neither one can exist there, and there is no sin in the wholly sanctified soul, either actual or inbred. It can't remain there, that is the home of the Holy Ghost. In the heart of the wholly sanctified is where the Holy Ghost lives, and He won't stay in the heart mixed up with either actual or inbred sin. So we see that the wholly sanctified man is a type of Heaven.

Again, we see that the Bible teaches a triune

God—Father, Son and Holy Ghost. And we have a kind of trinity of devils; we have to fight the world, the flesh and the devil. But we have God the Father to overcome the world with, and we have Jesus to overcome the devil with, and we have the Holy Ghost to burn out the flesh.

Again, we have the trinity of graces brought out in the Book. Paul says, "And now abideth faith, hope and love, these three, but the greatest of these is love."

And again, we have a trinity of evils brought out by John. He says, "Love not the world, neither the things that are in the world. If any man love the world, the love of the Father is not in him. For all that is in the world, the lust of the flesh, and the lust of the eyes, and the pride of life, is not of the Father, but is of the world. And the world passeth away, and the lust thereof: but he that doeth the will of God abideth forever." (1 John 2: 15-17.)

Here you see the lust of the flesh, and the lust of the eye, and the pride of life—there is a trinity of evils, but thank God! over against them we have the trinity of graces, and the blessed Christ said, "Greater is He that is in you than he that is in the world," and, "They that be for us are more than they that be against us." And Rev.

Seth C. Rees says that if the devil throws rocks at you, pile them up until you have a pile high enough to walk into Heaven on, and so, instead of the rocks a-hindering you, they will be turned into stepping-stones to enter Heaven on. And when you get to the top you can look back down the golden stairs that you have gotten to Heaven on, and shout through all eternity because the devil threw rocks at you while you were on earth, for, in doing so, he enabled you to gather material together to erect your stairs whose top reached Heaven.

We read in the blessed Book that we are to eat supper in Heaven, but nothing is said about breakfast or dinner. We have all talked much of going to the Marriage Supper of the Lamb, and, thank God! I am on the way to-day and the battles and struggles will soon be over. Now let me tell you about these three meals. We go through the long, dark night of sleep and, at the breaking of the day, we arise and prepare our breakfast —that is the first meal of the day. And then we go to work and work until high noon, and the great, old dinner-horn blows and we go to our dinner—that is our noon meal. And then we go out and labor all through the long afternoon, and at the setting of the sun the day's work is done, and we come in and eat our supper, but it comes after the day's work is done.

Well now, think of it in this light. Here is a poor, lost soul a-wandering in the dark night of sin; on and on he goes for several years, but finally he drifts into a meeting, he hears the preacher preach the unsearchable riches of Christ, and he is scripturally converted, he repents, confesses, forsakes his sins, and the light of Heaven breaks in on his soul. He is brought out of darkness into the marvelous light and liberty of the sons of God, and he receives the witness of the Spirit that his sins are all forgiven and that he is adopted into the family of God. Now, brother, that is that man's spiritual breakfast, his conversion is his breakfast, the first meal of his spiritual day.

Then he works on until noon, and he hears the dinner-horn of full salvation. He is by this time hungry and thirsty for the fulness of the Gospel of Christ, and he goes to dinner, and, behold, his spiritual dinner is the baptism with the Holy Ghost. He is, here and now, wholly sanctified, and that is the spiritual dinner, and on the strength of that meal he goes out and enters the harvest-field and toils all through the long afternoon of life, and at the setting of the sun

his day's work is done. His day here represents
his life's work, and it is now finished, and the
sun rolls behind the hills and pulls the mantle
over his day's work, and now the poor, tired
toiler steps into the chariot of the Lord and goes
sweeping through the gates into the city of light,
and on up to the Marriage Supper of the Lamb.
That makes his third meal, he eats two of them
on this side and the third one on the other side;
when he is converted, he has his breakfast, and
when he is sanctified, he has his dinner, and when
he is glorified, he has his supper.

That makes the threefoldness of salvation,
and it also gives us but the two works of grace
in this life. It seems that God has provided for
the human family the birth of the Spirit and the
baptism with the Spirit, and that seems to be all
that we need in this world, and that is all that
I can find that God ever promised the human
family in this world. All the new theologies and
new light and new baptisms and new gifts and
new revelations, when they are put to the real
test of life, all seem to be nothing but frauds.

I will go so far as to say this, no man knows
all that is included in the birth of the Spirit and
the baptism with the Spirit; just what we are
saved from we don't know, and just what we were

saved to we don't know, for no man knows the
depth and power of sin and no man knows the
height and power of grace. It takes the great
God to know the awful power of sin, and when
we have been in Heaven ten million years we
will still be amazed at the unfolding of human
redemption. In Rom. 11: 33, Paul says, "O the
depth of the riches both of the wisdom and knowledge of God! how unsearchable are His judg-
ments, and His ways past finding out!" When
the battle-scarred warrior looked into human redemption, his heart overflowed, and behold, the
above text was left written on a sheepskin.
O man, man, don't tell me that I haven't a good
thing!

Some men deny all of the wonderful exper-
iences that God gives to His children, and they
seem to think that knowledge will die with them,
but in that they are mistaken, for knowledge is
like the wind, any man can use it that can catch
it, and no man can catch it all, for which we ought
to be thankful. But thank God! I have caught
enough of the wisdom and knowledge of God to
climb out of the pit of sin, to swing around the
curve, and bridge the river, and tunnel the mountains, and some sweet day I expect to sit down
on the banks of the river of life. My disappoint-

ments will be changed to His appointments, and
the battles with the devil will be a thing of the
past, and the struggles with sin will all be over.
Each man will receive his own; the hidden things
of darkness will be brought to light and the right
man will go to the right place, and honor will
be bestowed on them that ought to have it, and
it will be the day of rewards, and all accounts will
be settled on that wonderful day of all days, for
it is said, "The great day of His wrath is come,
and who shall be able to stand?" Well, the Book
says, "He that hath clean hands, and a pure
heart; who hath not lifted up his soul unto vanity,
nor sworn deceitfully. He shall receive the blessing from the Lord, and the righteousnness from
the God of his salvation." This is the heritage
of the children of light. Well, Amen! That
is all that an honest man can ask or want or expect, and it just suits me. Glory to God in the
highest, and on earth peace, and good will toward
men, forever and ever. Amen!

CHAPTER XII.

The Blameless Life.

Dear ones, I want to talk to you about the blameless life. We read in 1 Thess. 3:13: "To the end He may stablish your hearts unblameable in holiness before God, even our Father, at the coming of our Lord Jesus Christ with all His saints."

It was the desire of the heart of the apostle that the Christians in the city of Thessalonica should be stablished, and that their lives should be blameless, and so he took the above text to lead them up to the experience of holiness, in order that they might be stablished. The stablishing blessing is just simply the blessing of sanctification, and without that there is no such thing as a stablished Christian.

If we read the first eleven verses of the first chapter of Romans, we will see at a glance that Paul was a-writing to Christians, and when he reached the eleventh verse he said, "For I long to see you, that I may impart unto you some spir-

itual blessing, to the end He may stablish your
hearts," or, to make it just as it reads, he says,
"For I long to see you, that I may impart unto
you some spiritual gift, to the end ye may be
established."

Now these Romans were Christians, and they
were in need of a blessing that would stablish
them. Now you read this eleventh verse and you
get a reference from it, and it runs you to chapter 15, verse 29. Read that verse and Paul says,
"And I am sure that, when I come unto you, I
shall come in the fulness of the blessing of the
Gospel of Christ." And that verse gives you
another reference, and that runs you back to the
first chapter and the eleventh verse, so we see
that the thing that they needed to stablish them
was the fulness of the blessing of the Gospel of
Christ. So we see that a justified believer is not
what the Bible calls a "stablished Christian."

We see also in the writings of the apostle
James that he is very clear on the subject. James
says (1:8): "A double minded man is unstable
in all his ways." Now we have before us a
double-minded man, and the next question to
settle is, Who is the double-minded man? Is
he a Christian, or is he a sinner? If he is a sinner, he has two minds in him, and if he is a Chris-

tian, he has two minds in him. Well, I am going to take the ground that the double-minded man is a justified Christian, from the fact that there are only two minds in the world, that is, the carnal mind and the mind of Christ. The sinner has but one mind in him, and that is the carnal mind; we all know that the sinner has not got the mind of Christ in him, but a justified Christian has got the mind of Christ in him. He already had the carnal mind in him, and that makes him the double-minded man, for when the sinner was born once he was born with the carnal mind in him, and when he was born the second time he was born with the mind of Christ in him, and that proves that he is the double-minded man.

And James says that the double-minded man is not stablished, so there is a justified Christian that the apostle James says has got two minds in him, and he says that he will have to get rid of one of them before he can be stablished. Now the question to settle is, Which one of the minds is he to get rid of? Well, we can settle that in short order. If he gets rid of the spiritual mind he will have no salvation left at all, and that will bring him right back to the place that he started from, an unregenerated sinner, but if he gets rid of the carnal mind, that will leave the mind of

Christ in him to reign without a rival. That was
the thought of both Paul and James, that the
double-minded man was to get rid of the carnal
mind, not keep the thing down, but "knowing
this, that our old man is crucified with Him, that
the body of sin might be destroyed, that henceforth we should not serve sin, for he that is dead
is freed from sin."

Again we read, in Jas. 4:8, this remarkable
statement: "Draw nigh to God, and He will draw
nigh to you. Cleanse your hands, ye sinners;
and purify your hearts, ye double minded." Now
the reader will notice that the above quotation is
much stronger and also much clearer than the
one in the first chapter and the eighth verse. In
the first chapter and the eighth verse he only
speaks to one class, and that was the double-
minded, but in the above text he addresses two
classes in the one verse, the sinner and the
double-minded, showing to the satisfaction of all
Bible readers that the double-minded man is not
the sinner, for he says: "Draw nigh to God,
and He will draw nigh to you," and then he says
to the sinner to cleanse his hands, and then he
says to the double-minded man for him to purify
his heart.

Well, here is the idea; if the sinner cleanses

his hands of his sins, he will be a double-minded
man, and if the double-minded man gets his
heart purified, he will be a single-minded man.
The sinner is carnal throughout his whole being
and has but the one mind in him, and that is the
carnal mind, but when he is converted and born
again he receives the mind of Christ. He already had the carnal mind in him, and that made
him two minds, and he then and there became a
double-minded man. But now he gets his heart
purified, the "old man" is crucified and he becomes
a single-minded man, the spiritual mind reigns
in his heart without a rival, and he is spiritual
throughout his whole being.

That was the idea of the two holy apostles,
and it should be the idea of every preacher on
the face of the whole earth to-day.

James said another good thing. He said,
"Pure religion and undefiled before God and the
Father is this, To visit the fatherless and widows
in their affliction, and to keep himself unspotted
from the world." A spotted cow or a spotted
sheep would make one think of Jacob's crooked-
ness, but. a spotted church-member would make
one think of a political grafter, so, beloved, we
had better look after those spots and see that they

are every one removed by the blood of the Son
of God.

But we turn again to our text and look at
the next thought, and we see what he meant by
the blameless life. The word unblameable is a
very high standard, but we know that God delights in high standards, and we also know that
the devil delights in low standards, and you can
tell-by a man's standard just about where he is
in divine things.

But if we only had this one text in the New
Testament on the subject of the unblameable life,
we might think that it was a mistranslation, as
we are told by the scholars that a few mistrans-
lations have crept into the Holy Scriptures, but
when we look close, we find so many texts on the
subject that we are convinced that the above text
is just as our Father wanted it, for He says, "To
the end that He might stablish your hearts unblameable in holiness before God." The man is
to be stablished in the state of holiness, and the
condition that he is to be in is blameless.

Now we read, in Luke 1: 6: "And they were
both righteous before God, walking in all the
commandments and ordinances of the Lord,
blameless." The reader will notice that in the
above text we have two that were righteous and

blameless, it says that they were both in that condition, that was the mother and father of John
the Baptist, so when we see the kind of parents
that John had, we are not surprised that the
world is still a-hating him and the true followers
of Christ are still a-naming their children after
him.   We also read, in Eph. 1 : 4: "According
as He hath chosen us in Him before the foundation of the world, that we should be holy and without blame before Him in love."   Here we see
that it was God's choice that we should be holy
and without blame before Him in love.   Now we
can't think of God making a choice for us and
making it down on a level with this old world.

But we notice again, in 1 Thess. 5 : 23, "And
the very God of peace sanctify you wholly; and
I pray God your whole spirit and soul and body
be preserved blameless unto the coming of our
Lord Jesus Christ.   Faithful is He that calleth
you, who also will do it."

The above text says that we are to be sanctified, and then preserved blameless, and kept in
that condition until Christ returns to this earth
again, and the text says that the whole man is
to be in that condition.   In many places where I
go they tell me that they are saved only in their
soul, and that their bodies commit sin every day,

both in word and in thought and deed. That is indeed a very strange combination, a saved soul in an unsaved body! And right in the face of such teaching, the above text says that your soul and spirit and body are all three to be sanctified wholly and preserved blameless, and kept in that beautiful state until the return of the Lord.

And again, the apostle Paul says, in 1 Cor. 6: 18-20: "Flee fornication. Every sin that a man doeth is without the body; but he that committeth fornication sinneth against his own body. What? know ye not that your body is the temple of the Holy Ghost which is in you, which ye have of God, and ye are not your own? For ye are bought with a price: therefore glorify God in your body, and in your spirit, which are God's."'

In the above text we notice first that "every sin that a man doeth is without the body," and we notice second that "your body is the temple of the Holy Ghost," and we notice third that "ye are to glorify God in your bodies and in your spirit, which are God's." Now, reader, if your soul is the Lord's and He wants to sanctify it, and He can do it, I see no reason why He should not do it. And again, if your body is the Lord's, and he wants to sanctify it, and can do it, I see no reason why He should not be allowed to

do it. If it is His, and He says that He wants
to sanctify it, what right have you to put in
a protest? If the body is the Lord's, and He
wants to cleanse it and make it holy, and live
in it, we have no choice in the matter, and
the Book proves that very thing. Look at 1
Cor. 6: 15: "Know ye not that your bodies are
the members of Christ? shall I then take the
members of Christ, and make them the members of an harlot? God forbid." Now here
is a text that takes the ground that our bodies
are the members of Christ.

Now in connection with the other text, look
at 1 Cor. 3: 16, 17: "Know ye not that ye are
the temple of God, and that the Spirit of God
dwelleth in you? If any man defile the temple
of God, him shall God destroy; for the temple
of God is holy, which temple ye are."

Now, he don't say that the soul of man is
holy and the rest of the man unholy, he says that
the whole man is holy, and, more than that, he
says that your whole body is the temple of God,
and is to be sanctified and preserved blameless,
and that God Himself is to live in your body
and make it His home in this world, and, in fact,
that is the only house that God lives in. He
isn't in the great temples that are made with

brick and mortar; He may go into a few of them, but it is only in the bodies of His saints that He dwells.

We will now give you one more Scripture to prove all the others by. Please turn to 2 Cor. 6: 16: "And what agreement hath the temple of God with idols? for ye are the temple of the living God; as God hath said, I will dwell in them, and walk in them; and I will be their God, and they shall be My people."

Here we have the statement that we are the temples of the living God, and that He, the living God, is to dwell in us, and walk in us, and He is to be our God and we are to be His people. Now, beloved, if that is true, and if that is the test of Christianity, and if nobody only those that have the living God a-dwelling in and walking in them are Christians, then we are in what is called a Christian age almost without a Christian in it. We are in a nation of more than ninety million people and sixty million of them non-professors, and of the thirty million that we have that belong to the different churches probably not one out of every hundred was ever truly born again; as a people they know nothing of the new birth or the baptism with the Holy Ghost, and the indwelling Christ is to them a joke and not a reality. They are taken into the churches by card-signing and by nothing but water baptism, and that is as far along as the most of the American church-members have ever gone. And yet we are said to be the leading Christian nation on earth, with plenty of large churches in plenty of the leading cities with a thousand members in them, and possibly not one member that was ever truly regenerated and born again. To preach a blameless life to them is as an idle tale; they are still blind to all that is worth having and they see no need of a clean heart. The one that they now have will let them dance and play cards and go to the shows and theaters and belong to all the lodges in the country, and they think that they have the best time in the world, and what is the use of getting a clean heart? They see no need of it. They are told that if they are baptised by immersion and belong to the Church, they are Christians; and if they are, they think that is enough to get to Heaven, for they think that Christians go to Heaven; and they do, for which I do praise the Lord.

But the last text quoted says that we are the temple of the living God, and that He is to dwell in us and walk in us, and that we are to be His

people and that He is to be our God.   Now if that
is what we are to have, we are a small band and
badly scattered over a large country, and our
leaders are few, for there are comparatively few
leaders in the religious world that seem to know
anything about a Christian experience that fills
a man with the Holy Ghost.   But thank God!
we have a few among the many, and those that
we have are worth more to the world than all the
others combined.   A preacher that is a-preaching to the suffering humanity around about him
that God is able to blot out all of their sins, and
then to baptise them with the Holy Ghost and fire
and take up His abode in their hearts, is doing
more than he knows to stem the tide and beat
back the oncoming tide of worldliness and darkness that is brought about by the preaching of
tens of thousands of preachers that are a-preaching that their people are on the road to Heaven,
when they are mixed up with everything in the
world that is worldly and devilish.   So, beloved,
if we get to that city in the skies, we have to
have more than water baptism, and we have to
have more than church membership; we must
be born of the Spirit, and we must be baptised
with the Spirit, and the living God must live

and walk in us and comfort us by the way, and that He will do, bless His holy name!

Well, remember the text, and remember the writer. The text says: "To the end He may stablish your hearts unblameable in holiness before God." He never said "before the folks," for a man don't always know how to judge, but God does. King Solomon said, "Will not the Judge of the whole earth do right?" Of course He will, and it is His will and plan and purpose for you and me that we should be holy men and women, and that our lives in His sight should be blameless.

CHAPTER XIII.

Repentance: Dangers In Neglecting It.

Dear reader, we want to talk to you about the doctrine of repentance and the dangers of neglecting it. You will turn to Acts 3: 19, and see what the apostle said on this important subject: "Repent ye therefore, and be converted, that your sins may be blotted out, when the times of refreshing shall come from the presence of the Lord."

The reader will notice three things in this text: first is a command, God said, "Repent;" and the second is a promise, if you will repent, your sins shall be blotted out; and the third is a danger-signal, God said for you to repent when the times of refreshing come from the presence of the Lord. Here is the danger, when the times of refreshing come from the presence of the Lord, it is easy to repent, and when the times of refreshing are not manifested and the Spirit is not working with men, it is hard work to succeed in doing anything that even looks like religion. When the saints of the Lord come to-

gether and pray and believe and expect the Spirit,
He is there to help in the work, and He will
refresh the saints, and He will put sinners under
conviction, and He will enable them to repent,
and the Spirit will help them to confess, and He
well help them to forsake their sins, and He will
help them to believe on the Lord Jesus Christ.

Repentance is a godly sorrow for sins, and
it means that I am sorry that I sinned; not just
merely sorry that I have been caught up with,
but a deep, godly sorrow that settled down over
me until I saw that I had sinned against God and
grieved Him by my disobedience. And a convicted man comes humbly to the throne of grace,
and there he finds grace to help him in time of
need, and if any man ever came to a time of
need, it is the man that has come to the foot
of the cross for mercy with a load of guilt on his
soul, and with nothing to offer God but misery
and sorrow and poverty, and conscious of the
fact that he is hopelessly lost unless God under-
takes his case. And this will He do, for God
never turned a penitent sinner away without giving him pardon and deliverance from all his
sins, and then giving him the sweet peace of pardon and the conscious knowledge of the fact that
he was a saved man.

But the danger-signal of the text suggests the thought that a man might be convicted, and he might reject the light, and he might say "No" to the call of mercy, and he might rise up and stubbornly resist the pleadings of the Holy Spirit. In so doing there is his great danger that is held out in the text as a danger-signal, for we find it on record that man has rejected light until hope fled from him, and he was left in his own darkness and sins, without one ray of light or hope; the Book teaches that a man may do that. We read, in Gen. 6: 3, where the Lord said, "My Spirit shall not always strive with man." There is a warning to man to not let the Spirit strive with him until He is grieved away. How hopeless is the man on this earth when the Spirit of the Lord has left him, to return no more!

Again we read, in Prov. 1 : 24-31 : "Because I have called, and ye refused; I have stretched out My hand, and no man regarded; but ye have set at nought all My counsel, and would none of My reproof: I also will laugh at your calamity; I will mock when your fear cometh; When your fear cometh as desolation, and your destruction cometh as a whirlwind; when distress and anguish cometh upon you. Then shall they call upon Me, but I will not answer; they shall seek Me early, but they shall not find Me: For that they hated knowledge, and did not choose the fear of the Lord: They would none of My counsel: they despised all My reproof. Therefore shall they eat of the fruit of their own way, and be filled with their own devices."

The above quotation is a fearful picture of somebody that crossed the dead line and could not return. The picture could not be darker than it is. If the great God will condescend to come down on a plain with man in his lost condition, and take sin out of his life, and lift him up on a plain with Himself, where God and man can have companionship with each other, and man rejects God's offer, there is no other court of appeals; he is just simply cut off. What hope is there of a man when he rejects God's love and mercy and says "No" to the call of mercy? A man that the Holy Spirit comes to and convicts has the power within himself to say "No" to God and reject everything that God offers him. If he has not that power, then he is not a free agent, and if he has that power, then he is on awfully dangerous ground. When God calls and he says "No," he is then and there taking the reins in his own hands and saying "No" to God right

to His face. God may call for man to-day and
man may not answer, and then, later in life, man
may call and God may not answer. If God calls
and man answers, then when man calls God
will answer; that is fair play, that is equal rights
to all men and special rights to none.

But after all, the fearful picture before us
is of a man that God refuses to talk to. That
side of it is too dark to look at, but it is true
nevertheless. But that is not all the Scriptures
that teach that man has the power to resist until
God leaves him in a hopeless condition. We next
turn and read Hos. 5:6: "They shall go with
their flocks and with their herds to seek the Lord;
but they shall not find Him; He hath withdrawn
Himself from them."

Here is the picture again of somebody that
woke up to the fact that they were lost, and they
went with their flocks and their herds to seek
the Lord, but they could not find Him, for He
had withdrawn Himself from them. In the long
quotation from Proverbs, we had God a-seeking
man and man could not be found, and in the
last quotation we have man seeking God and
God can't be found.

We next notice, in 2 Chron. 36:14-16:
"Moreover all the chief of the priests, and the

people, transgressed very much after all the abominations of the heathen; and polluted the house of the Lord which He had hallowed in Jerusalem. And the Lord God of their fathers sent to them by His messengers, rising up betimes, and sending; because He had compassion on His people, and on His dwelling place: But they mocked the messengers of God, and despised His words, and misused His prophets, until the wrath of the Lord arose against His people, till there was no remedy."

The reader will see at a glance that the above picture is a very dark one indeed. It shows a people that had everything on their side, and at the same time lost all. They did not live in the backwoods and never hear of the God of Israel, but they lived in the burning and shining light of the glory of Israel, and the priest was sent unto them from the Lord, and they knew their duty and did it not, so we read that the wrath of the Lord was kindled against His people till there was no remedy. They just simply rejected light until they were graduated in guilt.

As we look around us to-day and see the multitudes a-going in the same direction, it makes us tremble, for we see the other end of life, and we know that the wrath of a sin-avenging God

will overtake them like a mighty whirlwind, and
that swift destruction will be their reward, for
"the wages of sin is death." One of the crimes
of this age is the sin of rejection, but we say
with the apostle, thank God, "the gift of God
is eternal life through Jesus Christ our Lord!"

But we turn to see another text that teaches
us that man may say "No" to God one time too
often. We read next in Jer. 7: 14-16: "Therefore will I do unto this house, which is called
by My name, wherein ye trust, and unto the place
which I gave to you and to your fathers, as I
have done to Shiloh. And I will cast you out
of My sight, as I have cast out all your brethren,
even the whole seed of Ephraim. Therefore pray
not thou for this people, neither lift up cry nor
prayer for them, neither make intercession to
Me: for I will not hear thee."

If it were possible, this text is a little darker
than either one of the others. Here is a people that have gone in rebellion against God until
He tells us not to pray for them, and not to lift
up cry nor to make intercession for them, nor
prayers, for He says, "I will not hear thee."
There is the picture of a people that God so far
removed out of His sight that He would not even
allow anybody to make intercession for them,

for said He, "I will not hear thee." Well, He
meant by not hearing them that He would not
answer their prayers, and that their intercession
would have no effect on Him. There is no way
out of the thing, they had rejected God and His
word and His messengers until God's mercy had
been withdrawn from them and there was no
remedy. Their case was a hopeless one, not one
ray of hope ever overshadowed their pathway;
despondency was written over their heads, an
eternity without God stood out before them like
a great mountain range, their eternal destiny was
written across their hearts as plain as the handwriting that Daniel read to Belshazzar; their
doom was sealed.

While that was so of these God-rejecting
Israelites, that is the condition to-day of tens of
thousands of our American church-members.

The text for this discourse said, "Repent ye
therefore, and be converted, that your sins may
be blotted out, when the times of refreshing shall
come from the presence of the Lord." Mark
you, beloved, He did not say, "Repent any time
that you think best." He said, "Repent when
the times of refreshing shall come from the presence of the Lord." It was then or never. They
were not consulted and asked what time would

it suit them to repent. God said for you to repent when the times of refreshing come, and not
at the time that it will suit you best. When God
said to us "Repent," He meant for us to do it;
and when God said to us to "Come," He meant
for us to come to Him and receive just what
He had to give us, and God is never empty-handed
when He calls a fellow; and when God said "Go,"
He meant for us to start at once; and when God
said, "Woe" to us, He meant for us to stop at
once.

Well, we will just give you one more text to
show you that we may not hearken, and we may
not repent, and we may reject, until we are cut
off from the presence of the Lord forever and
ever. We now read, in Zech. 7: 11-13: "But they
refused to hearken, and pulled away the shoulder,
and stopped their ears, that they should not hear.
Yea, they made their hearts as an adamant stone,
lest they should hear the law, and the words
which the Lord of hosts hath sent in His Spirit
by the former prophets: therefore came a great
wrath from the Lord of hosts. Therefore it is
come to pass, that as He cried, and they would
not hear; so they cried, and I would not hear,
saith the Lord of hosts."

There are a number of remarkable statements in the above quotation. First, "but they refused to hearken;" second, "and pulled away the shoulder;" third, "stopped their ears" in order that they might not hear the law; fourth, "they made their hearts as an adamant stone," that they might not hear the law and the word that the Lord sent them by His Spirit by His former prophets; fifth, there "came a great wrath from the Lord;" sixth, "therefore it is come to pass, that as He cried, and they would not hear; so they cried, and I would not hear, saith the Lord of hosts."

As far as we can see, these people did all that a people could do in order that they might not be saved. It looks like they had their minds made up to be lost in spite of all that God could do or would do.

Oh, beloved, when God said, "Repent, and be converted, that your sins might be blotted out, when the times of refreshing shall come from the presence of the Lord," it meant a great deal more than many men think. It is a command from the Lord, and it is as binding as if He said, "Ye shall not steal," or, "Ye shall not kill." When He said, "Ye shall not take the name of the Lord thy God in vain," He meant it; that was one of His binding commandments, and it stands out

to-day before a perishing world, but He also
said, "Repent, and be converted," and that also
is one of His binding commandments. And if a
man will hearken to this commandment, he will
keep all the others, but if he don't hearken to this
one, there is no need of his keeping any of the
others, for they won't have any effect on him, and
will count for nothing at the judgment bar of God.
Suppose a man does, in a sense, keep a few of the
commandments and refuses to obey this one,
what would they be worth to him? The first
thing that God requires at the hand of a sinner
is to repent of his sins, confess them out to God,
get them put under the blood of the blessed Son
of God, and receive the witness of the Spirit that
his sins are all forgiven and that his name is
written in the Lamb's book of life; and then he is
prepared to keep all the rest of the commandments. The Lord God only knows the joy that
will come into the life of a man that repents of
his sins, and while that is true, the great God is
the only one that knows what sorrow and horror
will settle down over the man that refuses to
repent and holds on to his sins. Just what it will
mean at the Judgment will not be known to mortal
man until he stands there in the presence of God
and hears Him say, "Depart from Me, ye cursed,

into everlasting fire, prepared for the devil and
his angels." So, beloved, you had better get busy
and repent at once; don't let the sun go down on
you and find you out of the ark of God's love and
mercy. Rise up in your God-given power and by
the aid of the Spirit, repent of all your sins, go
through with Jesus, and land on the shores of
eternal deliverance; claim God's promise. He
says if you will repent that your sins shall be
blotted out, and just now I can hear my blessed
Christ say, "Come unto Me, all ye that labor and
are heavy laden, and I will give you rest. Take
My yoke upon you, and learn of Me; for I am
meek and lowly in heart: and ye shall find rest unto your souls. For My yoke is easy, and My burden is light." An easy yoke always makes a
light burden.

Well, may the blessings of Heaven rest upon
all who may read this little note of warning, and
may it help somebody to stop before they cross
the deadline, and the love and mercy of God are
forever turned away.

But remember that He loves us to the end,
and, as long as there is any hope, He never turns
us over to the devil. But see the crowd that Paul
describes in Rom. 2: 5, 6: "But, after thy hardness and impenitent heart, treasurest up unto thy-

self wrath against the day of wrath, and revelation of the righteous judgment of God; who will render to every man according to his deeds." The above picture is a description of a man that just simply refused to repent, and his heart got harder and harder and he drifted farther and farther away from God each day of his life, until the closing day, and we have the above picture. The heart was hard and it was also impenitent, and then, to add to the fearful condition, he was treasuring up wrath against the day of wrath and the revelation of the righteous judgment of God. This is not a very pleasant picture to hang on the wall, but if we can see it in time to make our peace, calling and election sure with God, we will shout over it for millions of years in the city of God. Well, Amen! Let's meet at the Marriage Supper of the Lamb, and talk over matters. It will be much easier to understand there than here, and we can make the landing if we want to worse than we don't want to.

CHAPTER XIV.

NECESSITY OF CONVERSION AND SANCTIFICATION.

Dear reader, I want to talk to you for awhile on the necessity of being converted and then wholly sanctified. The text for this message will be found in John 3: 3 and Heb. 12: 14. First we will notice John 3: 3: "Jesus answered and said unto him, Verily, verily I say unto thee, Except a man be born again, he cannot see the kingdom of God." And now in connection with the above text we give you Heb. 12: 14: "Follow peace with all men, and holiness, without which no man shall see the Lord."

Now the reader will see at a glance that there are two things that a man will have to have to make his home in Heaven, the first is the new birth and the second holiness. The reader will see that the joy of salvation is not our theme, or the beauty of a life of holiness. There is great joy connected with salvation from all sin, and the life of holiness is one of the most beautiful things in the world, but we will leave the joy of it and the beauty of it to you to enjoy. It is the necessity of it that we will talk about in this discourse.

Now we turn first to Heb. 9: 27, and read: "And as it is appointed unto men once to die, but after this the Judgment." Now here we see that men are to die and then go to the Judgment, so you see at a glance the great necessity of not only being converted, you see also the necessity of being sanctified wholly, cleansed from all sin, and filled with the perfect love of God, for the Judgment Day will be the day of all days.

Now the reader will remember that we are told by many of the great leaders of the religious world that there is no resurrection of the wicked, and that only the righteous will be resurrected, but if you will turn and read Acts 24: 15, you will see that their teaching is not Book at all, but a trick of the devil to damn lost men. See what the apostle says about it, and see if you can afford to go with the false teachers. "And have hope toward God, which they themselves also allow, that there shall be a resurrection of the dead, both of the just and unjust." Here we have both classes at the Judgment, the just and the unjust, one class as well as the other, and each one is there for his reward, whatever it is, whether it is eternal life or eternal death.

Both companies are there, and each man is rewarded according to his work, so if there is no resurrection for the wicked, there is no resurrection for the righteous, and if the wicked is not rewarded for his works, the righteous will not be rewarded for his works.

In proof of that, we now turn to 2 Cor. 5: 10: "For we must all appear before the judgment seat of Christ; that every one may receive the things done in his body, according to that he hath done, whether it be good or bad."

Here again the reader will see both classes at the Judgment, and he also will see both classes there for the express purpose of receiving their rewards for whatever they have done, whether it be good or bad. So we have both classes still together. The reader will see that the separation has not come yet, but all hands are there, and all hands are concerned, and each man will receive what is a-coming to him. This is one court where no bribing will be heard of, no place here to buy off a death sentence, for the eternal destiny of each man will be in the hands of the Judge of the whole earth, and King Solomon said that the Judge of the whole earth will do right. When I see a drunken bum leave the court-room, and hear him swear and curse and

tell the rest of his crowd that he did not get
justice, I always know that he did not, for if he
had, there are ninety-nine chances to each hundred that he would have gone to the chain-gang
instead of back up town, and I know of some
large cities where every officer of the city and
also the mayor, if they had justice, would be in
the "Pen" to a man. But you will understand
that their day is a-coming. God's eye is on them,
their hairs are all numbered, the death angel
is on their track and their days are numbered,
and every step taken in wrong-doing has been
seen by the All--seeing Eye. There each man is
to face his own record, and will be rewarded according to his works.

When we look at the above text, we see, as
never before, the great necessity of being born
again, and also of being made holy, for there is
nothing that will stand the test but the birth of
the Spirit and the baptism with the Spirit; we
must have both.

Now in the next text we will look at one that
takes up the sinner without the Christian at all,
and shows him as he will stand. The reader
will notice that the texts that we have quoted were
all to both sinners and Christians, but in Rom.
2: 5, 6, we have a text that is addressed to the

sinner: "But, after thy hardness and impenitent heart, treasurest up unto thyself wrath, against the day of wrath, and revelation of the righteous judgment of God."   And then the sixth verse says that God "will render to every man according to his deeds."

The reader will see that in the fifth verse is a fearful picture of the man that says "No" to the call of mercy and hardens his heart. The apostle said, "But, after thy hardness and impenitent heart." You will see that after the heart becomes hard and impenitent, then he begins to treasure up wrath against the day of wrath, and the man that has nothing to look forward to at the Judgment Day but the wrath of a sin-avenging God has a picture before him that is enough to make every angel weep and every demon in the pit blush and hang his head, and it is enough to make every sinner on earth scream against the skies until he hears from God and the angels come with full pardon and a complete redemption from all sin.

We next notice that God has the day already appointed. We turn to Acts 17: 31: "Because He hath appointed a day, in the which He will judge the world in righteousness, by that Man whom He hath ordained; whereof He hath given assurance unto all men, in that He hath raised Him from the dead." Here the apostle tells us that the day is appointed, and he takes the ground that the fact that God raised Jesus from the dead is the proof that He will bring us all to the Judgment. He makes the resurrection of Jesus the basis on which He will resurrect all other men and bring them to the general resurrection, both the wicked and the righteous.

But some may say, "What is the use of having a general Judgment Day? ·If the wicked goes to a place of punishment when he dies, and if the righteous goes to a place of rest, why should they be brought from their places and judged and rewarded? Well, there is a reason for so doing. In the first place, when a wicked man dies he may go to a place of punishment, and he does, but he cannot at the time of his death be judged and rewarded, from the fact that his work is not done at his death; in fact, it has just begun. All of the above text says that we are to be judged according to our works, and the beauty of a life of righteousness is seen in the fact that the work goes on after the worker has gone on to his rest, and the fearful side of a life of sin is seen in the fact that his life of sin goes on after he has gone to a place of punishment to await the general

Judgment Day, in order that God may reward him for what he has done on earth.

Now take the case of John Wesley on one side and Voltaire on the other. It would have been impossible for God to have rewarded John Wesley when he died, from the fact that his work had just begun. Look at the millions of people that have been blessed by the life of John Wesley since he died. We read in Rev. 14: 13: "And I heard a voice from Heaven, saying unto me, write, Blessed are the dead which die in the Lord from henceforth: Yea, saith the Spirit, that they may rest from their labors; and their works do follow them." Here the reader will see that the works of the children of God go on after they go to their rest, therefore they could not be rewarded at the time of their death, from the fact that their works are not done. John Wesley has had a greater influence in the world since he died than he did before his death. His life is to-day felt throughout the whole world, and all the people that have been blessed since John Wesley died will be put down to his credit, or at least he will have an interest in the work that was done through his life and influence.

And take John Knox, for instance, and see what he has done for the world, and see what

his credit will be at the general Judgment Day.
Take Martin Luther, and see if you can count the
interest on what he invested for God and a lost
world. "They do rest from their labors, but their
works do follow them."

And now take the case of Voltaire, and Tom
Paine, and others that lived in sin, and rejected
God, and fought everything in the known world
that looked like goodness, and see their life and
its influence on the world. Every man that has
read their works and turned infidel, God will put
down to their credit, and they will have to give
an account to Almighty God at the Judgment
Day for every soul that they damned with their
life and influence, and they have damned more
since their death than they did while they were
living. So they are not resting from their labors,
but they are to-day in sorrow, and there is no
rest for them day or night, either in the body or
out of the body; they are wretched and miserable,
and when the Judgment Day is come and they
meet their works just as they have done the
things, then God can judge them and reward
them according to their works. So we see at a
glance that they could not be rewarded until their
work is done, and their work will go on until
the general Judgment Day.

On that day the work of men will be completed, so far as their influence for either good or bad is concerned, and at that day the final separation will take place, and never, while eternity rolls on, will either ever meet up with the other again. After that great day is over, no Christian will ever see another sinner, and from the close of that day no sinner will ever put his eyes on another Christian. They are in the same country to-day, and the Christians are a great bother to the sinners; it makes them mad for us to even speak to them about the salvation of their souls, but it won't be long until they will never be bothered with us again, they will have their own way and will be allowed to go on in sin and take their fill of sin, with not one person to ever speak to them about their soul, for they will be lost and there will be no one to bother them about salvation.

We have the final separation brought out in Matt. 25: 46: "And these shall go away into everlasting punishment: but the righteous into life eternal." Here the separation is final; one goes one way and the other goes the other; one up and the other down; one into the light of Heaven and the other into the darkness of outer darkness; one with the good and the other with the bad;

each one goes to his own place, each man has made his choice. The old Book said that "the wages of sin is death," and one man made his choice and took sin; and the old Book said that "the gift of God is eternal life," and one made his choice and took eternal life. Each man is laying up for the other world, and whatever he lays up will be there awaiting his arrival; if it is good, it will be there; if it is bad, it will be there.

It will be natural, it seems to us, for each man to want in his death what he wanted in life. Here is a man that loved God and holiness and righteousness and Holiness songs and Holiness meetings and Holiness testimonies, and the fellowship of the Holiness folks was his delight on earth, and I am of the opinion that when he comes to die that nothing on earth would please him like a fine band of Holiness folks to come to see him and stay with him until he crossed over, and while he was a-passing to have them sing and pray and testify and praise the Lord and read the Word of God.

Well, now, let's apply that to the other side, and see how it will look. Here is a man that has no use for God, and he hates Holiness people, and he hates Holiness preachers, and he never at-

tends church, and he curses them all every time
he thinks of them, and he loves drinking and
swearing and gambling, and cardplaying, and
fighting, and the drunkard and the harlot are his
companions. But he is now on his death-bed, and
of course it looks like he would want his crowd
around him when he was a-passing from this
world.   But just think of it! here is a poor sinner
in a dying condition, and he is without God, and
he has no hope, and the gamblers and drunkards
and the harlots gather around him, and as the
darkness of eternity begins to settle around him,
and he can feel the awful pains of death as they
reach for his heart-strings, and the drunken mob
can see at a glance that he is dying, one of the
gamblers throws down a ten-dollar bill, and says
to one of the mob, "I will bet you ten dollars that
Jack is dead and in Hell before ten o'clock to-
night!"   He cries, out of the agony of his soul,
and says, "Oh, men, don't do that! I am a-dying
and I am lost!"   And the mob begins to make
fun of him, and they mock him, and one of them
says, "Oh, yes, old pard, you're a-showing the
white feather," and then they give him "an awful
gag" (as they call it) and one of the big, rough
fellows steps up and throws down twenty dollars,
and says, "I will bet you twenty dollars that Jack

don't go to Hell before ten-thirty to-night!" And about this time the whole mob begins to gamble over the dying sinner. Some bet that he will be in Hell by nine-thirty, and others bet that he will live until ten, and still others put up their money that Jack will live till eleven, and the man that bets on him a-living the longest runs to his bottle of liquor and brings it to poor, dying Jack, and says, "Old pard, here is some of the best whisky in this town, and I want you to drink with me for the last time. I am betting fifty dollars that you don't go to Hell before eleven o'clock to-night. Come on; here, don't go back on me. You must drink it or you will die, and I am a loser; you must drink this liquor." And the poor, dying sinner groans out an awful wail, and says, "Oh, men, don't do that! I can't drink, I am dying!" But they grab him, and pull his head up, and one of the mob pulls his mouth open, and they get the liquor-bottle to his mouth, and he is too weak to swallow it, and they pour it down him, and he strangles to death, and they all give him an awful cursing.

The day following they are to bury Jack, and they have his grave dug, and his coffin brought, and when they put him into the coffin he is a little too long, but they push him down into the coffin and give it an awful cursing, and take him out to the grave, but it is not quite long enough, and they get upon it and stamp it down into the ground, and curse the grave, and the coffin, and curse each other, and wind up with a big fight at the grave.

Now, sinner, there is your choice, that is what you say that you want. Well, man, take that and go with it forever and ever, but let me die the death of the righteous, and let me have his reward, and let me stay where he stays in this world and where he stays throughout eternity. Sin is moral insanity, and every sinner on earth is morally insane, and is under the delusion of the devil and is led by him captive at his will.

CHAPTER XV.

Dear reader, I want to talk to you about the four confessions, of which two were made under the old dispensation and two under the new. The first one was made by Pharaoh, king of Egypt. We read in Ex. 10: 16: "Then Pharaoh called for Moses and Aaron in haste; and he said, I have sinned against the Lord your God, and against you."

Now the reader will notice this confession; it was straight and clear and to the point. He said, "I have sinned." No man can make a better confession than the one that was made by Pharaoh. But some one will say, "Well, Brother Robinson, if Pharaoh made as honest a confession as any man could make, why was he destroyed in the Red Sea?" Well, that is no trouble to answer at all. Now if you will turn to Prov. 28: 13, you will see just why Pharaoh was destroyed

244

after his honest confession. Notice the reading of this text: "He that covereth his sins shall not prosper, but whoso confesseth and forsaketh them, shall have mercy." You notice that King Solomon went farther than Pharaoh went. Pharaoh said, "I have sinned," and he stopped there, but Solomon said, "Whoso confesseth and forsaketh them, shall have mercy." We see that Pharaoh confessed his sins, but we also see that Pharaoh held on to them until they put him in the bottom of the Red Sea and ran an ocean of red water over him and his braves with their horses and chariots. They went down with a mighty crash and an awful wail, just like all other sinners that hold on to their sins.

To confess your sins is a long step in the right direction, but that is not enough, you must go away out and beyond that; you must confess them and then forsake them. Pharaoh had taken the first step, but he failed to take the second, and with his honest confession he was lost, and was no better off in the bottom of the Red Sea than he would have been if he had not have made any confession at all. He went farther than plenty of good people go nowadays; he not only confessed his sins, but he went so far as to ask for prayers, and said to Moses, "When you and the men go out in the wilderness to have a men's meeting, pray for me."

I am of the opinion that Pharaoh was a lodge man; he was willing for Moses to have men's meetings, but he did not want the women and children to go. But Moses was not at all a lodge man, for he said, "Our wives and our little ones shall go with us."

And Pharaoh said to Moses, "Pray ye to the Lord for me, that none of these things come upon me that ye have mentioned; for I have sinned," and then he added, "The Lord is righteous and I am wicked." But after all of the confessions that he made, he still held on to the old life of sin until it destroyed him and his people.

It is a fact that you may go to any sinner in the country, and say to him, "Are you a sinner?" and he will smile and say, "I am the worst man in town," and he will go on to say, "Why, man, you don't know how bad I am; I am a terror to the country," and while he tells you how bad he is, he is a-laughing and seems to think it funny, and takes it all as a common joke. But Pharaoh was in real earnest, and at the time he was under conviction and really wanted help from the Lord, but when it came to the real test, he went back on all of his convictions, and also on his confession. But poor Pharaoh! he held on to his sins a little too long; they damned him before he ever turned them loose. What a pity that a man with the brain that Pharaoh had would hold on to this old world until it was his ruin!

But now we turn to another noted character that stands out very prominent in Old Testament history—that of Achan. We find, in Josh. 7: 20, these words: "And Achan answered Joshua, and said, Indeed I have sinned against the Lord God of Israel, and thus and thus have I done."

The reader will notice that Pharaoh said, "I have sinned," and Achan said, "I have sinned." They both made the same confession, but both held on to the things of this old world until one went to the bottom of the Red Sea and the other went down under a shower of stones and was left under a great pile of rocks.

The catching of Achan was a wonderful piece of the unfolding of the divine mind. Achan was hidden out among at least three million of people, and it would have been impossible for Joshua to have found out the guilty party, but God sort of arranged a pre-arranged judgment day, and instead of the great God Himself a-sitting on the throne, He put Joshua on the throne, and had him to carry out the plans of the Lord, and in so doing Achan was caught and punished.

God's plan to catch Achan was to have Joshua to bring out all the tribes of Israel and have them to pass by Joshua, tribe by tribe, and the Lord told Joshua that when the tribe that had the guilty man in it came by He would notify him, and that Joshua was to send all the other tribes to their tents and only keep the tribe with the guilty man in it. And so here they come, tribe by tribe, tribe by tribe, and the tribe of Judah was taken, and all the others were allowed to go to their tents. And now the families of Judah were taken, family by family, and then they were taken household by household, and then they were taken man by man, and in a short time they had caught the guilty man, and God's command was that he and all his family must be burned with fire and a great heap of rocks piled over them. And God called the valley where this man and his family were stoned and burned and left under a great heap of stones, the valley of Achor.

The reader will see that Achan made an honest confession; he said, "I have sinned," but he held on to the wedge of gold, and the shekels of silver, and the Babylonish garment until it took the lives of thirty-six of his brethren and his wife and all of his children. Oh, the danger of sin; how fearful it is! The reader will notice that the sin of Achan did not just affect him, but look at the harm that it brought to others that were innocent and had nothing to do with the crime of Achan. So we see that it is impossible for a person to sin without hurting some one that is innocent.

I have heard the Democrats and the Republicans say, "Oh, well, if you will let liquor alone, it will let you alone," but that is a lie as black as the crime of Achan. I have seen mothers and wives that never touched liquor, but it robbed them of their husbands and sons, and of their home and food and clothing and everything on the earth that was worth living for, and yet they had let it alone all the days of their precious lives. Look what it has done for them, and see if the statement made is a true one, that "if you will let liquor alone, it will let you alone."

Achan might have said the same thing, but just turn and look, and behold we see thirty-six dead men, all brought about by the sin of Achan, and turn and look again, and behold yonder go the wife and children of Achan to the valley of Achor to die for the crime of the husband

and the father, and to be burned with fire and then left under a great heap of stones.

Well, somebody may say, "Oh, well, it is not right for the innocent to have to suffer with the guilty." That is true, and if Achan's wife was a true Christian woman, she went to Heaven, but if she wanted her husband, Mr. Achan, to get the beautiful Babylonish garment for her, she was damned with her husband, and they went down together. Of course if their children were small and innocent, they were saved, but we don't know their ages or anything about their conduct, and we leave them in the hands of the Lord, and King Solomon said, "Will not the Judge of the whole earth do right?" and we say, "Yes, of course He will."

We are not uneasy about the Lord, but we are a-trembling for the folks that are a-dabbling with sin, and when we see this Government a-selling licenses to the saloon men of this country, to come right into your community and wreck every home, and rob the mothers of their sons and daughters, and rob the wives of their husbands, and take the bread out of the mouths of the children, and yet the nation just laughs at it, we are made to not only tremble, but we quake and fear for them, for just as sure as God caught

and punished Achan, He will catch and punish
every man in this nation that is guilty of the
above crimes. They confess that it is evil and
bad, but for the same cause that Pharaoh and
Achan held on to their sins until they were both
damned, this Government is a-holding to the
filthy lucre until it will wreck and then damn this
nation. Great God! wake us up before we get
into a red sea of the wrath of a sin-avenging
God, and before we are called to meet God in the
valley of Achor, and there face the shower of
stones and the on-coming torch of the wrath of
a just God whose laws have all been broken and
whose grace and love and mercy rejected and
spurned.

God caught Pharaoh and Achan, and they
both had to face their own conduct, and we will
not escape if we neglect so great salvation. God
has provided a remedy for all sin and unclean-
ness, and it was sufficient to meet the demand
of both Pharaoh and Achan, but they both rejected it. A few shekels of silver got over their
eyes and blinded them, until they saw nothing
but gold and silver and the finest of the raiment
of this old world, but how cheap are these things
to-day to either one of them. If they just had
one more chance, they would accept it, but the

last chance came to them both; they both rejected
it and lost their golden opportunity for a little
of the gold of this world, and in a few fleeting
days lost the gold of this world, and then they
had lost both this world and the one to come.

We now turn to the New Testament and see
the confessions that were made there. We first
turn to Matt. 27: 4, and read the confession of
Judas. Here it is: "Saying, I have sinned, in
that I have betrayed the innocent blood. And
they said, What is that to us? see thou to that."

We here have the same confession made by
Judas that was made by Pharaoh and Achan.
Notice, Pharaoh said, "I have sinned," and
Achan said, "I have sinned," and Judas said,
"I have sinned." Oh, those three words, how
fearful they look!—I HAVE SINNED.

No man that ever walked the earth had a
better chance to get to Heaven than Judas; he
was one of the twelve apostles, he was called and
commissioned and sent out by the Master Himself, he heard every sermon that the Son of God
preached, he saw every miracle that Jesus ever
performed, he was there and heard every parable
that Jesus ever spoke, he was on hand when
Jesus blessed the bread and fish and fed the multitudes, he was there when Jesus walked on the

water, he was there when Jesus spoke to the raging waves of Galilee and said, "Peace, be still;" he was there when Jesus cast the devils out of the man, he was there when Jesus said, "Lazarus, come forth," and he saw Lazarus get up and walk out of the tomb; and then, in the face of all he saw and knew, he sold out the Master for a few shekels of silver, and he held on to them until they burnt his flesh like fire.

Oh, the power of silver! What harm it has done to this old world in that it has robbed men of their precious, immortal souls, and then robbed them of Heaven, and then put them into the pit and left them there forever to brood over silver while eternity rolls on.

Poor Judas! How near he was to Heaven, and yet went down. Think of Judas and the dying thief. The dying thief was almost lost, but yet saved, and Judas was almost saved, but yet lost. Judas had thousands of opportunities and lost them all, and, as far as we know, the dying thief only had one and he accepted that one. As far as we know, the dying thief never saw Jesus until they were all nailed to the cross, and as he hung there by the nails that went through his hands to hold him to the cross, he looked over and saw Jesus for the first time, and

the face of Jesus broke his heart, and he said,
"Lord, when Thou comest into Thy kingdom, remember me," and Jesus said to him, "To-day
thou shalt be with Me in Paradise."

But while the dying thief was a-trusting the
Lord for salvation, Judas was a-preparing to take
back the money. And now you behold Judas
as he makes his way back to the priests. He
rushes into their presence and utters the text:
"I have sinned, in that I have betrayed innocent
blood." But poor Judas! he got no comfort from
the priests, they only laughed in his face and
said, "What is that to us? see thou to that."

Oh, beloved, how little comfort there is in this
old world! They will get you into an awful,
heart-breaking trouble, and then, when you go
to them for comfort or aid, they will mock you
to your face, and laugh at you and make fun
of you right to your face, and say, as did the
chief priest, "What is that to us? see thou to
that." This old world will do you all the harm
possible, and then shift all of the responsibility
back on you. Nobody on earth but a true Christian ever bears any responsibility; a true Christian will load up himself with all the troubles of
everybody in the country, and bear them all
through life, but not so with this old world; see

how little comfort Judas got. The money that
he sold his Lord for is now burning his flesh
like fire, and when the mob of God-forgetters
and Christ-despisers begins to laugh in his face
he throws the money down in the hall, probably
at the same place where they paid it to him just
a few hours ago, and now he starts out to end
his life. He is now disheartened, and it is not
long until despondency settles down over him,
and the next stage is despair, and the next step
is death, and the next one is damnation.

See the devil's ladder—Disheartened, Despondency, Despair, Death and Damnation. That ladder never fails to reach the pit; that is the most
successful run to outer darkness that a sinner can
travel; he never fails on this road, he is just
as sure to make the landing as he gets on the
road and keeps on traveling.

And now Judas has bought his rope and he
is looking for a good place to finish the job, and
the devil is there to help him hunt the place, and
Judas and the devil soon found the right place;
it was a large olive-tree a-standing on the edge
of a high cliff. And now Judas asks the devil
how to proceed, and the devil knew just what
for Judas to do next. He was to get up into the
tree, and get out on a limb that overhung the

cliff. You see the devil was a-going to have Judas to make it safe, so that if one thing failed the other would succeed. So now you behold Judas out on the limb overhanging the cliff, and one end of the rope around the limb and the other end around his neck. Now we see Judas as he sits there on the limb, and he begins to meditate upon the last three years of his life, what golden opportunities he has had, and now they are all gone; what wonderful privileges he has enjoyed, but now they are all gone. Every sermon that he has heard comes up before him, the spotless life of the Christ is now a-standing out before him, the fellowship with the other apostles comes up before him, and from where he is sitting on the limb no doubt but he can see Mt. Calvary and the Son of God on the cross. He sees the mob of folks as they hurry from Jerusalem to Calvary, and from Calvary back to Jerusalem; he can hear the victorious shouts of the mob, and about the time that darkness begins to settle down over Jerusalem he can hear the dying groans of the thieves, and he listens, and he finally hears the last words of the Christ, as He cried out, "It is finished!" and just as Christ gave up the ghost and bowed His head, Judas leaps off of the limb and down his body goes to

the end of the rope, and the crash was so fearful
that the rope broke, and down over the cliff goes
the flying man, and worse still, the dying man,
and worse still, the lost man.

"I have sinned" is a fearful testimony. Oh,
reader, don't let that be your last testimony! You
see that every sin goes under the Blood, that
every step is ordered of the Lord, that every
act of your life is seasoned with the salt from the
King's table. Go nowhere that the Holy Ghost
is not free to go with you, and be caught nowhere
that you would be ashamed to be caught if Jesus
were to come in the clouds.

Dear reader, we will now take up the last
confession, and you will find it to be the same
as the other three, only while the first three confessed and held on to their sins until they were
ruined, the last one confesses and forsakes and
finds the Pearl of greatest price.

We now look at the confession of the Prodigal
Son. It is found in Luke 15: 18: "I will arise
and go to my father, and will say unto him,
Father, I have sinned against Heaven, and before thee, and am no more worthy to be called
thy son: make me as one of thy hired servants."

Now let the reader just think of these four
confessions: Pharaoh said, "I have sinned," but

he held on to them until they put him in the bottom of the Red Sea; and Achan said, "I have sinned," but he held on to them until they burnt him with fire and put him under a great heap of stones; and Judas said, "I have sinned," but he held on to them until they put the rope around his neck and swung him off of the olive limb, and then down over the cliff, and out into outer darkness; the Prodigal Son said, "I have sinned," but notice, he next said, "I will arise and go to my father, and will say to him, Father, I have sinned, . . . and am no more worthy to be called thy son: make me as one of thy hired servants."

You will find the Prodigal Son made two confessions, he made one in the hog-pen and got up and left the hogs and started home, and he made the other when he got home, or when he met his father. The hog-pen is a type of sin and the first confession is a type of the sinner a-forsaking the life of sin. This boy did not say, "I have sinned," and then remain in the hog-pen. He said, "I have sinned, and I will arise, and will go." See the difference between him and the other three? He said, "I have sinned, and I will arise, and I will go to my father;" the other three said, "I have sinned," but they stayed with

their sins until they were destroyed. But the
Prodigal said, "I have sinned," and the next thing
you see he is over the fence, and he is leaving
the swine herd behind him. We read, "He came
to himself," and we read another thing also, we
read that when he had spent all, a mighty famine
arose. You see the famine did not arise until
all was gone; that is always the case, as long as
you have plenty, there is no famine, and could
not be, but when the last nickle was spent the
famine had just arrived, and as he fed swine
and lived on husks, he thought of his father's
house. The colored man said the meaning of that
little statement "he came to himself" is that he
left with plenty, and he spent all his money, and
then he sold his overcoat and spent that, and then
he sold his dress-coat and spent that, and then
he sold his vest and spent that, and then he sold
his top-shirt and spent that, and then he sold
his undershirt and spent that, and then he came
to himself; yes, sir, he had got to the hide then,
nothing else now to sell. Well, the old darkey
is a great philosopher, after all.

But thank God! the Prodigal Son did not stay
in the hog-pen after he came to himself, he started
home, and we read that his father saw him when
he was a great way off, and ran to meet him,

and as they met the son began on the second
confession, and got to make it only in part, for
before he got through with it the father fell on
his neck and went to kissing him, that was the
kiss of reconciliation, and he ordered the servants to bring forth the best robe and put it on
him, and a ring and put it on his hand and
shoes on his feet.

Now, the Prodigal Son's return is a type of
the return of the backslider. He had been in
his father's home before, but had left and had
wasted all. That is the experience of every backslider. They have been to their father's house,
and they have wandered away and have gone to
feeding the devil's swine, and they are in the
hog-pen, or, in other words, they are down in
a life of sin. But the father had never forgotten
his wayward son, but the memory of him still
lingered with the old father. You will notice
the words of the father after the son got back
and the kiss had been planted on the boy; he
said, "Bring forth the best robe, and the ring,
and the shoes, and let the fatted calf be killed,
for this my son was dead and is alive again, he
was lost and is found," and .they began to be
merry.

Now the above texts all go to show the two

works of grace; first, the son confessed; and second, he forsook; and third, he left the hogs; and fourth, he got to his father's house; and now the father had compassion on him, and ran and met him, and fell on his neck, and kissed him. There is the kiss of reconciliation, the father and son were reconciled. Next notice, now the father had the best robe put on him, there is a robe of righteousness; next he put the ring on his hand, there he sealed it with the seal; next he put the shoes on his feet, there he was shod with the preparation of the Gospel of peace. Now, the kiss and the robe and the ring and the shoes must represent pardon, reconciliation, being clothed, sealed and shod.

Well, now you say, "Where is the second blessing?" Well, that is what we are now about to come to. Now we read that the Father said, "Bring forth the fatted calf." Now the object of a feast is to get full. The killing of the fatted calf is the feast that was to follow the kiss and the robe and the ring and the shoes. If the kiss and the robe and the ring and the shoes don't represent pardon, there is nothing in the Bible that does, but thank the Lord! we know that they do, for the old father said, "This my son was dead, and is alive again." You will please no-

tice the words, "Alive again, was lost and is
found." That makes a good New Testament
Christian out of him, and now the killing of the
fatted calf and the feast and the music and the
dancing all go to show the fulness of the blessing of the Gospel of Christ. That all took place
after the father said that he had received him safe
and sound, and safe and sound goes to show
that the conversion was a thorough one and a
perfect work of grace, and that all prepared the
Prodigal Son for what was to follow, and that
was the killing of the fatted calf and the feast.
Well, Amen! I say, Glory to God for a salvation from all sin for all men, forever and ever!

CHAPTER XVI.

The Dying Testimonies of the Three Rich Men of the New Testament.

Dear reader, I want to talk to you about the last testimonies of the three rich men of the New Testament.

We only hear of three rich men in the New Testament, and they were all three lost. That is a warning to us to listen to the words of our blessed Christ. Through the apostle Paul he tells us to set our affection on things above and not on things on the earth. (See Col. 3: 2.)

The first testimony that we will look at is in Matt. 19: 22, and we also have the same testimony in Mark 10: 22, and also in Luke 18: 18. This is the Rich Young Ruler. Matthew said that when he heard the conditions of eternal life he went away sorrowful, for he was very rich; and Mark said that he went away grieved, for he had great possessions, and Luke said that he was very sorrowful, for he was very rich.

When this young man came to Jesus, it looked

like he was a hopeful case.   St. Mark said of the
young man that when he came to Christ he came
a-running and kneeled to Him.   Now, reader,
there is earnestness for you, and humility, the
things that not many have got, but this young
man had both.   And when he got to the Savior
he said, "Good Master, what shall I do that I
may inherit eternal life?"   And Jesus said to
him, "Why callest thou Me good? there is none
good but One, and that is God."   Then Jesus
added, "Thou knowest the commandments," and
as Jesus named them, the young man listened,
and said to Jesus, "All these have I kept from
my youth, what lack I yet?"   And Jesus said
to him, "If thou wilt be perfect, go sell all that
thou hast, and give to the poor, and come, and
take up the cross and follow Me."

At a glance, you can see where the young
man broke down.   The young man said, "What
lack I yet?" and Christ said, "If thou wilt be
perfect, go sell all that thou hast, and give to
the poor, and come, and take up the cross and
follow Me."   "Go sell all that thou hast, and give
to the poor," is the place where Jesus caught up
with the Rich Young Ruler.   Luke said that he
was very rich, but he was interested in the salvation of his soul, for he ran to Jesus, and went

forward for prayers in the middle of the street, or on the public road. Mark said that he kneeled to Jesus; that is, he got down on both knees, he was under deep conviction and went forward for prayers, and was in earnest, and he expected to go through. He had no idea that Jesus would put him to such a test as He put to him. "Sell all," was the test.

Notice, now, what followed; "and he went away grieved, for he had great possessions." But Mark said that "Jesus, beholding him, loved him," but for the riches of this world he went away, and we never hear of him again. The last mention that is made of this young man was that he went away sorrowful, we never hear of him again. We will see him some day, but he will be a-going away sorrowful when we behold him.

It don't look possible that a man would go forward for prayers, and get down on both knees and ask the Master what he was to do to inherit eternal life, and see the conditions, and then back out, but this man, and millions of others, have done the same. The most of men go away sorrowful when they hear the Master's conditions. "Sell all, and follow Me" is putting it too hard and straight for the most of men. It was the wealth of this old world that stood between that young man and his eternal destiny. It would have been ten thousand times better for him if he had been a pauper, for if he had he would have been in Heaven to-day, but as he was very rich, he is a lost man. If a man will follow the dark trail of sin through this country, he will find that the crimes of this age are brought about by the love of money, for the apostle said, many, many years ago, that the love of money was the root of all evil. How sad is the case of this young man! But compare him with the young men of this age, and you will find them all in the same condition; no hope, no salvation, no Christ, no Heaven, and the great bulk of them even without any morality. The average young lady in the average city in company with the average young man is just as hopeless as a lamb would be fifty miles from the city on a dark night in a herd of wolves. No thinking man would believe for a minute that the lamb would ever escape. Oh, the black track of sin!

How inviting this old world looked to that Rich Young Ruler, but where is he to-day? what is his outlook to-day for a good time? He will not be seen again on the streets of this city, he is gone, and he went away sorrowful, and he is still a-going away; he hasn't stopped since he turned his back on the Master. There is no stop to sin, it goes on forever and ever. Unconfessed sins never die; they have crossed oceans, rivers and mountains and sat on the footboard of the bed to torment the dying sinner. There is but one remedy, and that is to confess and forsake them.

Now, reader, we will turn and look at the next testimony. It is found in Luke's Gospel, the twelfth chapter and twentieth verse: "But God said unto him, Thou fool! this night thy soul shall be required of thee." We read of this man, that he was very successful in his business; he made a very great fortune and raised so much that he had nowhere to put it, and he finally did a wise thing, and the thing that he did was good and right, no harm in it, and it was not wicked at all; he just looked around him and saw that he had more stuff than he had room for, and he thought within himself to know just what to do with all his goods and his fruits, and he said, "Well, I will do this: I will pull down my old barns, and build greater ones; and there will I bestow all my goods and fruits." But now listen to the next statement, "and then will I say to my soul, Soul, thou hast much goods laid up for many years; take thine ease, eat, drink, and be merry."

Now, reader, notice that last clause, "take thine ease, eat, drink, and be merry." The mistakes of this man are before us. He got his mind on this old world and forgot his eternal destiny; he was so busy a-raising fruit, and tearing down barns, and erecting larger ones, that he let the time slip, and death overtook him, and behold! he was not prepared to meet it, but God said unto him, "Thou fool! this night thy soul shall be required of thee." Because this man got his mind on this world and its goods, and neglected his immortal soul, God called him a fool, and yet he was a very bright fellow, and he stood well in the community. He was not dull in the fact that he did not know anything, he was well posted and well informed, and in his business he was up to date. His motto was, "Business is business, and it is my business to do business," but he saw so many grapes that he failed to see God, and he craved goods so bad that he had no taste for salvation; he wanted this world so bad that he did not want Heaven; he was so interested in his stomach that he forgot his soul; when he got his barns all full he was a pauper. He said, "Soul, eat," but God said, "Soul, die;" he said, "Soul, be merry," but God said, "Soul, come to the Judgment;" he said, "Soul, take thine ease," but God said, "Soul, go into outer darkness."

Oh, beloved, don't let this man's fate be yours. Turn from this old world, flee to the cross and see the bleeding Lamb before it is too late, and before you hear God say to you, "Thou fool! this night thy soul shall be required of thee." Don't get your eyes on fruits and barns and forget God and your precious, immortal soul.

Now put the testimonies of these two men together. Notice, they read like the testimony of one man. First we read that he turned away sorrowful, and second, "But God said unto him, Thou fool! this night thy soul shall be required of thee." Now, reader, there is the last testimony of two men, and yet it makes up the testimony of one man. He "turned away sorrowful"—"To-night thy soul shall be required of thee;" that is the natural order, if they take the first step, they are compelled to the second one. When you turn away from the Lord, the next thing will be a death-bed horror and a Judgment scene, and the last wail of the soul that was lost. If you turn away here, He will turn you away there. The chief business of man is to look after

his soul. The affairs of this life are a secondary
matter, and by no means should they have the
first place in the life of a man. It has been wisely
said that "man needs but little here below, and he
needs that little but a short time," for the old
Book said, "For here we have no continuing city,
but we seek one to come, whose Builder and
Maker is God," and the apostle Paul said to us,
"Set your affection on things above, not on things
on the earth. For ye are dead, and your life
is hid with Christ in God. When Christ, who is
our life, shall appear, then shall ye also appear
with Him in glory. Mortify therefore your
members which are upon the earth." And then
he proceeds to tell us what we are to do in order
to be at our best in this world, but the Rich
Young Ruler and the Rich Business Man both
got so entangled with the affairs of this old world
that they could not break loose from it, and it
bound them and held them in such chains of
bondage that it put them both in the pit.

As I travel over this country, I see the rich
young ruler and the rich business man every-
where I go, and they neither one have any time
for God or their salvation; they are as completely
consumed by this world as the two men described
in the last two testimonies. The love of money

has filled the state prisons, and the jails, and
the gambling-houses, and the brothels, and the
Sunday baseball parks, and loaded down the Sunday trains, and filled the streets with Sunday
newspapers. For the love of money men will
sell their souls, and women will sell their virtue.

Dear reader, we now turn and look at the
last testimony. We find it in Luke 16: 23: "And
in Hell he lifted up his eyes, being in torment."

Now, reader, if you will put these three testimonies together, you will have the testimony of
just one sinner as he dies without God and goes
out into the darkness of eternal despair. Now
put them together and see how it looks: first,
he turned away sorrowful; second, "this night
thy soul shall be required of thee;" third, "and
in Hell he lifted up his eyes." Now there is
the testimony of these three rich men, or, in
other words, we have before us the testimony
of the dying sinner, for the testimony of one
sinner is the testimony of all sinners.

We now have him in the final place of abode,
he is now in Hell. He first turned away from
the blessed, loving Savior of man, and then he
had not gone very far on the road until God
required his soul of him, and he was not ready
to meet the God that he had rejected; and the

last thing, we hear of him in Hell, and he lifted
up his eyes, being in torment.   But he had not
forgotten anything, his mind was as active in
Hell as it was in this country.   He still had his
memory, and all his past life stood out before
him as if it had been the day before, he remembered every opportunity, he remembered every
privilege that he ever had, he remembered every
Gospel message, he remembered every hymn that
he had ever heard sung, he remembered every
prayer that he had ever heard offered.   The
very day that he turned away sorrowful stood
out before him in letters of fire, and it will be
the fearful nightmare that he will ride throughout all eternity; it is the ghost that will haunt
him forever and ever, and as he lifts up his
eyes in Hell he will remember the day that he
turned away sorrowful, and the night that God
required his soul at his hand and he was not
ready will stand out before him, and he will say,
"Oh, if I had only said 'yes' to the whole will
of God; how different my life would have been!"

There is nothing like memory.   The unkind
word will stay with us like burrs in the sheep's
wool, it will be there until shearing time, no way
to get rid of memory.   The kind words and kind
acts and the good deeds will be in your mind

forever, and they will bring such joy to your
heart and life that you would not take a world
for them, but, on the other hand, just think of
a misspent life, the bitter oath, the drunken de-
bauch, the night of revelling, the day of theft,
the night of murder, the day of grafting, the
hour of hate, the day of malice, the unkind deed,
the life spent in sin, the fearful waste of time
and money, the loss of Heaven, the loss of your
precious, immortal soul, the opening of the black-
est world in the universe to receive you at your
coming! All of these things will stand out before you like great mountains, no way to hide
them; they must all be met and settled for, and
owned as your very own, and you will have to
keep them while eternity rolls on. There is but
one way to get rid of them, and that is to confess them, and forsake them, and repent of them,
and put them under the blood of the blessed Son
of God, and plead His dying groans as your only
hope, and let the Lord know that you are there
for business, and that you have come for mercy
and not for justice, for no sinner can meet the
justice of a sin-hating God. You must plead His
mercy and plead your need, for it is your need
that will recommend you to God, and not your
goodness, or your ability, or your greatness;

there is but one thing that commends us to God, and that is our helpless, dependent condition.

The three rich men were just as needy as any three poor men that could have been found anywhere on the face of the earth, but they loved the world, they loved the praise of men, they loved the association of sinners, they hated the association of God's children, they had no time for the Church of Christ, Sunday-school never entered their minds, the missionary cause never entered into their thoughts. They loved salvation only to the extent that it extended their business and brought them gain, they loved law only to the extent that they could use it to collect all that was a-coming to them and that it would protect their wealth and give them liberty to have a good time in the country where law was enforced. They would sell liquor as quick as they would sell family groceries to increase their wealth; they would rob the poor, laboring man of his last dime and see his little children go hungry for bread as quick as they would sell a piece of hardware. They were rich, and the Book says very rich, and had great possessions, but they were not in touch with God, they were out of harmony with the Bible, they hated everything that looked like holiness, they could not

bear to hear holiness spoken of, nothing grated
on their refined ear like the word "sanctification," it was perfectly disgusting to them, it was
one thing that they could not tolerate at all.

But alas! my brothers, the last testimonies
that this old world ever heard from you were
that first you turned away sorrowful, and the
next time we heard of you God had required
your soul of you, and the next thing that we
heard of you was that in Hell you had lifted
up your eyes being in torment, and the last
words that you spoke were a-pleading for one
drop of water.   How things had changed!

It don't look possible that a man so rich could
come down so low in the scale of poverty that
he could not get one drop of water, but so says
the old Book.   He said, "Please, father Abraham," but Abraham said, "Son, remember."   Oh,
that awful statement, "Son, remember."   Beloved, that memory of yours, what are you going
to carry around in your memory throughout all
eternity?   Will you have the sweet memory that
Jesus was offered to you and you accepted Him as
your Savior, or will you carry the fearful memory
around forever that you had the chance of a home
in Heaven but you said, "No, not to-night; no,
not to-night"?   That is the saddest word that

ever fell on the ear of the Son of God, but the most delightful word that ever fell on the ear of the devil was the word "Not to-night." It is always pleasing to the devil for men to put off the salvation of their souls till some further time, but how it grieves the heart of the Son of God! Oh, beloved, remember the testimonies of these three rich men and flee to the cross for pardon and purity.

CHAPTER XVII.

The Eye of God.

Dear reader, we want to talk to you for a little while about the eye of God.

As a people, we often speak of the All-seeing Eye. We mean by that that there is an Eye that never sleeps and is never closed, which is always on man and his conduct is never hid from the one that never sleeps. We read in 2 Chron. 16: 9: "For the eyes of the Lord run to and fro throughout the whole earth, to shew Himself strong in the behalf of them whose heart is perfect toward Him." But, in Gen. 16: 13, we read this remarkable statement, "Thou God seest me."

For a little while we want to look at this last text and think it over as we find it here in the Book. The text is the language of the Egyptian girl when she fled from the face of her mistress. She stopped by the fountain that was near Shur that was in the wilderness, and he spoke to the girl and asked her where she was going, and she told him that she had fled from the face of her

mistress, and when she found out that God was
a-watching her she called the place "Thou God
Seest Me."

Now, reader, if the people in the United
States could just realize that God sees them, they
would stop their crimes by the thousands, but
they have been so blinded by the devil that man
in this day can't realize that God is a-looking
at him.   What a change there would be in the
pulpit if every preacher in the United States
could just feel that God is a-looking at him.
If they could be woke up to that fact, preachers
would go to preaching on the doctrine of repentance until a revival would break out that
would shake the foundations of the kingdom of
the devil, and revivals would sweep this country
and men and women would be saved by the
millions.   But tens of thousands of American
church-members haven't heard a red-hot sermon
on repentance and death and Hell and the Judgment Day in many years, and as it is preached
but little, they have got out to the point that,
if they do happen to hear a man preach on the
subject, they think that because it is not preached
in their pulpit the fellow that does preach it is
a crank, and they discredit all that he may say
because it is not preached where they go to wor-

ship. But if it was thundered from every pulpit
in the land, "Repent and be converted, that your
sins may be blotted out when the times of refreshing shall come from the presence of the
Lord," and if they were to get tired of such
preaching and think to go to some other church
the next Sunday, and behold, the man of God
would walk into his pulpit and take for his
text, "Repent and be converted, that your sins
may be blotted out," and as they sat there and
listened to him as he showed them what it was to
be scripturally convicted and then what it meant
to repent of their sins, as they would sit there
and listen to the man of God as he showed him
that Bible conviction was the Holy Spirit opening their spiritual eyes to see that they were a
set of lost sinners and that repentance was a godly
sorrow for all sins committed, and that they must
be so sorry that they would repent of them and
never be guilty of committing those sins again,
and after repentance then comes the confessing
of their sins, and after confessing them the next
thing is to forsake them, and after forsaking
them the next step is to believe on the Lord Jesus
Christ and then and there their sins would all
be forgiven and the sweet peace of God fill their
hearts, and when that had taken place that they

would now be the justified children of God and
they would now be adopted into the family of
God and at that time would become the sons of
God—there is no doubt in my mind in the least
but if the multitudes of this country could hear
a few months of such preaching on repentance
and Hell and the Judgment that thousands of
the members of the churches would rise up and
get a good case of old-fashioned; heart-felt religion, and the churches would all have to be
enlarged, for they would not hold half of the
people that would want to go. It is no trouble
to get people to go to church where there is something a-going on, where the fire is a-falling, and
the saints are a-rejoicing, and sinners are a-weeping their way to the cross of Calvary, and are
a-finding the Pearl of greatest price.

If this was preached from every pulpit in
the land, a revival would break out in spite of
the devil, and their difficulties and their circumstances would have but little to do with it. A
pulpit on fire makes its own circumstances and
burns up its own impossibilities, and the thing
is on when the preachers of this country get
ready for it. I am thankful that we have some
men that are to-day a-preaching on repentance
and Hell and the Judgment Day and holiness and

the coming of our Lord, but to compare them to the great bulk of preachers that are not preaching on those special doctrines we have comparatively few, they are wofully in the minority.

It makes it very hard on a few men to face this hundred million of God-forgetting, fun-loving, worldly Americans, but if the world itself could just wake up to the fact that "Thou God seest me," it would scare them to death. The devil won't allow them to even think of the dreadful truths as we find them.

God sees every step that we take, and hears every word that we speak, and knows every thought that passes through our minds. There is not one sinner in a thousand but what, if he would sit down and just think over his life and his conduct and where he is a-going, and how long he will stay there, and who he will have to keep company with, for at least one hour, but who at the end of that time would be a Christian or a raving maniac; he would be ready for a place in the Church of Jesus Christ or he would be ready for a place in the madhouse. But you may say, "Well, why don't he do it?" Well, just simply because the devil has him so completely bound that the man is not allowed to think of such things. I have seen men just have

one serious thought and almost give up sin, but
the minute that a feeling of seriousness comes
over the sinner, the devil is there to bring a
thousand things into his mind and get his mind
on the affairs of this old world again, and drive
all the thoughts of the Judgment Day out of
his mind, and his precious, immortal soul is abso-
lutely in the hands of the devil, and he will not
let him think of Christ and the day of death
and the on-coming Judgment.

When such things come into the mind of a
fellow, the devil will tell him that he has plenty
of time yet, and that there is no use in the man
giving up all that is worth living for and becoming an old man while he is young; he will
say to have a good time and after while, when
it is really necessary, then there will be plenty
of time to serve the Lord.   And it all looks so
reasonable to the young man or the young woman
that they take it for granted that after they have
had a good time in the world that they will then
have plenty of time to serve the Lord and to make
their peace with Him.   But after while they find
themselves on their death-bed, and up comes the
devil and he is now the first one to tell them that
it is now too late, that they have put it off too
long, there is no hope for them in this world.

He will say that away back yonder the time was
when they could have repented of their sins and
have made peace with God, but that it is now too
late, their day of grace is forever gone.

The devil is a very great preacher, and he
has a mighty following in this country, they follow him by the millions, and over the earth by
the hundreds of millions. He is the preacher
of the age; but of course we know that he don't
preach the Gospel, and could not preach the
Gospel, for the Gospel is the power of God to
salvation to the Jew first and then also to the
Greek. We read the words of the apostle where
he says, "For I am not ashamed of the Gospel
of Christ, for it is the power of God unto salvation to every one that believeth, to the Jew first
and also to the Greek," or to the Gentile world.

If men in the political world could just realize
that "Thou God seest me," there would never
be another saloon licensed, or another gambling-
house licensed, or another house of shame licensed. No man would walk the streets of the
cities with a cigar in his mouth, no boy would
spend his money for cigarettes if he just could
realize that God was a-looking at him, and no
young lady would ever be caught at another ball
if she felt down in her heart that God was a-look-

ing at her.   She has killed her timidity, and her
modesty is all gone, and she has become brassy
and brazen and hard and wicked, but it is all
because she don't feel that God is a-looking at
her; if she really felt that God was a-looking
at her, she would feel like sneaking off and hid-
ing from the face of God, and never looking this
old world in the face again.   Poor child! she is
in the hands of the only enemy that woman ever
had, for if there was no devil, there would be
no enemy to the woman; he is her only enemy,
he has tried to destroy her ever since he found
her in the garden of purity and happiness, and
after he was the cause of her fall, and then after
the Lord had made her a promise that the seed
of the woman should bruise the serpent's head,
the devil then renewed his attack on the woman,
and it has been his dirty work to degrade woman
and put her down under the iron heel of man
and make her a beast instead of making her a
lady.

But the promise of God was fulfilled, and the
time came when the woman brought forth the
Man-child that was to run the devil down and
lock him up in the pit, and the seed of the woman
was the Christ.   Everybody else that was ever
born was called the seed of man, but the Christ

was called the seed of woman.   Man had nothing to do with the conception and the birth of
the blessed Christ, but it was man that put Him
to death, and it was man that put Him in the
grave, and it was man that stood around the
grave to keep the Son of God in the grave.
That was the only place that man ever saw the
blessed Savior that he was willing for Him to
stay.   They were so much interested in it and
they wanted Him to stay there so mighty bad
that they went so far as to put the Roman sol-
diers at the grave of the Son of God as guards
to keep Him in the grave.   The chief priest told
them to make the grave as secure as they could,
but behold, how faint they were when the angel
went down to roll the stone away; we read that
they all fell like dead men, and did quake and
tremble.   That is just a little bit of history to
let us know that God understands man, and that
man is not in the way of the Lord at all.

We get a glimpse of the weakness of man at
the grave of our blessed Lord, and oh, if we
only could get men to realize that God is as near
to them to-day as He was then, and just as
powerful, and sees them in all their conduct to-
day as He did the day that they laid plans to
keep His Son in the grave!   He saw their plans

and understood their whole scheme, all the work
that was done was to get rid of the Christ, they
did not want Him then and they don't want Him
to-day, but thank God He is on hand for the
few that do want Him!

But we next notice the first text that we
quoted, that "the eyes of the Lord run to and fro
throughout the whole earth, to shew Himself
strong in the behalf of them whose heart is perfect toward Him."   The reader will notice that
this text is addressed especially to the Holiness
folks, it is to them that have perfect hearts, or
whose hearts are perfect toward the Lord, and
to all such He says that His eyes are a-running
to and fro throughout the whole earth for the
express purpose of showing Himself strong in
the behalf of them whose hearts are perfect.
There is no such a text of Scripture anywhere
else in the Bible, this is the only text that says
that the Lord's eyes are running throughout the
whole earth.   It is in connection with the sanctified folks, those that have the blessing of perfect love, and to-day a holy man is the best-pro-
tected man in the whole world, nobody else on
earth like him, he is the only person in the world
that has such a promise behind him; there is

nothing in the Book to anybody else that reads like the text that we have behind us.

Will H. Huff says of such Scriptures that they give us something that is rock-ribbed to stand on, and we believe it. Glory to His name forever and ever!

How secure is any preacher that has the blessing of scriptural holiness, and that keeps his hand in the hand of God, and lives such a life that he knows that God's eyes are over him, and that God is behind him, and that his backing is as strong as the universe. How brave should a preacher be to declare the whole counsel of God with such backing at his disposal. How secure should the layman be that is in possession of the fulness of the blessing of Christ, and how brave and courageous should our statesmen be if they were the men of God. How they should stand for the righteousness of God and the good of the nation, for when God is behind a statesman he has the only backing in the universe that is worth having, everything else shall crumble and tumble and fall into decay and come to naught, but when we think of the man in any avocation of life that knows that the eyes of the Lord are over him, and that not only that but that His eyes are there in order to show Him-

self strong in the behalf of this very man, and as
long as that man lives that life and keeps himself
there His protection is as strong as the God of
the universe, how strong he should be.

That is the man that John the beloved had
in his mind when he wrote those beautiful words,
"He keepeth himself, and that wicked one touches
him not." And again, he is the same fellow that
the great apostle had in his mind when he said,
"He that doeth these things shall never fall."
Of course he won't, for all Heaven is beneath
him; the arms of the Lord are beneath the fellow, and God is able to hold him up. We read
in the Book, and I am believing it with all my
heart, that the Psalmist said that "The eyes of
the Lord are upon the righteous, and His ears
are open to their cry." He also said that "the
face of the Lord is against them that do evil,
to cut off the remembrance of them from the
earth." And how true that is, the wicked die
and are forgotten, but after the righteous have
been dead for more than a hundred or a thousand years, the good folks are still a-naming
their children after them.